50 YEARS

lonely  planet

OF TRAVEL

POCKET

LOS ANGELES

TOP EXPERIENCES • LOCAL LIFE

RYAN VER BERKMOES

Contents

Plan Your Trip   4

Welcome to
Los Angeles 4

Los Angeles'
Top Experiences 6

Dining Out 12

Bar Open 14

Treasure Hunt 16

For Kids 18

Responsible Travel 20

Active LA 22

Live Music 23

Beaches 24

Celebrity Spotting 25

Under the Radar 26

LGBTIQ+ Travelers 27

Four Perfect Days 28

Need to Know 30

Los Angeles
Neighborhoods 32

Hollywood Blvd
SEAN PAVONE/SHUTTERSTOCK ©

Explore
Los Angeles   35

Hollywood...........................37

Griffith Park, Silver
Lake & Los Feliz 55

Highland Park.................... 69

West Hollywood
& Beverly Hills....................77

Miracle Mile
& Mid-City...........................91

Santa Monica 107

Venice................................ 121

Downtown.........................137

Burbank
& Universal City 159

Worth a Trip

Malibu.............................. 168

Disneyland® Resort 170

Survival
Guide   177

Before You Go 178

Arriving in
Los Angeles 179

Getting Around 180

Essential Information ... 182

Special Features

Hollywood
Walk of Fame 38

Griffith Observatory........ 56

Getty Center..................... 88

Academy Museum
of Motion Pictures........... 92

LACMA 94

Venice Boardwalk 122

Broad................................ 138

Exposition Park.............. 154

Universal Studios
Hollywood........................ 160

Welcome to Los Angeles

Dreams are serious business in LA, a city where exuberance is encouraged. This is a place that mixes fantasies with hard realities, whether you're hoping to create your own fabulous future or you're a visitor hoping to taste the energy. It's a sprawling region of such diversity – in cultures, tastes and attractions – that it defies clichés. But like a blockbuster feature, it demands attention.

Downtown Los Angeles
© CHONES SHUTTERSTOCK

Los Angeles' Top Experiences

Go star spotting on the Hollywood Walk of Fame (p38)

SEAN PAVONE/SHUTTERSTOCK ©

Get in on the action on Venice Boardwalk (p122)

Enjoy amusement park fun on Santa Monica Pier (p108)

Plan Your Trip Los Angeles' Top Experiences

Learn everything about film at the Academy Museum of Motion Pictures (p92)

Find thrills with movie-themed fun at Universal Studios Hollywood (p160)

Marvel at the A-list art at Broad (p138)

Discover the stars at Griffith Observatory (p56)

Explore three great museums at Exposition Park (p154)

HAYK_SHALUNTS/SHUTTERSTOCK ©

ELLIOTT COWAND JR/SHUTTERSTOCK ©

Take in the wealth of art at LACMA (p94)

Don't miss the Disneyland® Resort (p170)

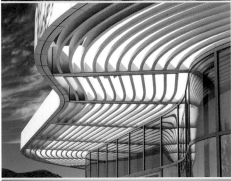

Admire the art and architecture of the Getty Center (p88)

Check out the beauty and beautiful people at Malibu (p168)

Dining Out

LA dining is a global feast. There's no shortage of just-like-the-homeland dishes, from xiao long bao to pupusas to waffles. Add in California's farmland bounty and you'll chew your way through your visit. Ever tried a gluten-free vegan donut with organic peach jam? LA may be many things, but a culinary bore isn't one of them.

The Big Shots

LA's homegrown visionaries range from Michelin-starred Michael Cimarusti (Providence and Connie & Ted's) to Nancy Silverton (Osteria Mozza). Others include Mary Sue Milliken and Susan Feniger (Border Grill and Socalo) and Bryant Ng (Cassia). Tetsuya Nakao (Asanebo) shows the strength of LA's Pacific-rim restaurants.

And this being LA, you can expect extra helpings of celebrity chefs. Shows like *Top Chef* and *Iron Chef* are stocked with local talent, including Brooke Williamson (Playa Provisions), Ludo Lefebvre (Petit Trois) and Tal Ronnen (Crossroads Kitchen).

Food Trucks

Some of the best bites in town come on four wheels, with mobile kitchens serving up a global feast of old- and new-school flavors. Track food trucks at Roaming Hunger (roaming hunger.com), or check the websites, Facebook or Instagram feeds of favorites like Kogi BBQ (kogibbq.com), Cousins Maine Lobster (cousins mainelobster.com), Mariscos Jalisco (@MariscosJalisco) and El Ruso (elrusola.weebly.com).

Best in Town

Providence Creative, meticulous seafood worthy of its two Michelin stars. (p45)

Cassia Smashing East-West fusion in Santa Monica. (p114)

Bavel Melds the flavors of Israel, Turkey, Egypt and Morocco. (p147)

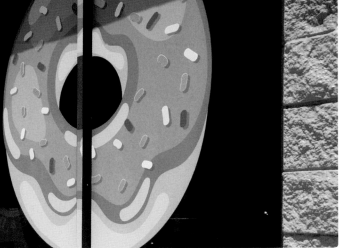

MIKELEDRAY/SHUTTERSTOCK ©

Orsa & Winston Fuses Asia and Italy in exquisite tasting menus. (p149)

Mother Wolf An ode to Rome in Hollywood. (p45)

Best Old-School LA

Canter's 24/7 kosher classics, a giant bakery and servers who have seen it all. (p100)

Musso & Frank Grill Direct from Hollywood's Golden Age. (p44)

Bob's Big Boy Googie diner within spitting distance of Warner Bros Studios. (p164)

Original Farmers Market Global flavors at an atmospheric 1930s landmark. (p100)

Best Cheap Eats

Trejo's Coffee & Donuts Brings Mexican flavors to beloved LA classic eats. (pictured; p46)

Joy Made-from-scratch, Taiwanese-inspired bites. (p71)

Tail O' the Pup LA-style hot dogs any way you want them. (p85)

Best Standout LA Bites

Gjelina Imaginative small plates made with top local produce. (p129)

Sonoratown Sonora-style tacos and burritos. (p148)

Grand Central Market Bustling hub of global LA-style street food. (p148)

Pearl River Deli Casual Cantonese has never been better. (p149)

Park it Yourself

Valet parking is pricey, and an additional $2 tip is customary. To save, try to find street parking, often available nearby or avoid the issue by taking the Metro or a rideshare.

Bar Open

Whether you're after a craft cocktail made in a style Bogie would have preferred or a saison brewed with oolong tea, LA pours on cue. From postindustrial coffee roasters to mid-century lounges, classic Hollywood martini bars to cocktail-pouring bowling alleys, LA serves its drinks with a generous splash of wow.

Specialty Bars

LA claims a growing number of specialty bars, focused on one particular libation. Small-batch coffee is the raison d'être at specialty coffee shops like Be Bright Coffee and chains like Intelligentsia, Verve and Maru, while wine bars like Covell in Los Feliz and Tabula Rasa in Hollywood's Thai Town have become bastions for niche and out-of-the-box vino. La Cuevita in Highland Park has a huge collection of agave. Silver Lake claims a dedicated sake bar in Ototo,

while the Japanese theme extends to Highland Park's Gold Line, one of a handful of LA bars inspired by Tokyo-style 'listening bars,' known for their sharply curated turntable tunes.

Cold Pressed

Southern California claims to have invented the fruit smoothie, but a much hotter recent trend is cold-pressed juice. While conventional juices are produced using fast-spinning blades to pulverize the produce, cold-pressed juices are made by

pressing the liquid. The process reputedly protects the juice from heat and excessive oxidation, resulting in a drink with a greater concentration of vitamins, minerals and live enzymes – or at least that's what they say in LA!

Best Specialty Bars

Varnish Superb cocktails in a secret backroom speakeasy. (p150)

Big Bar Experimental cocktails and off-duty bartender customers. (p63)

El Carmen Solidly stocked tequila and mescal tavern. (p102)

STEVEN A. MILLER/WIKIMEDIA COMMONS ©

Covell Around 150 wines by the glass. (p63)

Best for a View

EP & LP Cocktails and flicks with views of the Hollywood Hills. (p85)

Perch Vintage-inspired glamour atop a Renaissance Revival high-rise. (p150)

Upstairs at the Ace Hotel Downtown views and powerful cocktails. (p150)

Best for Beers

Homebound Brew Haus House brews in grand Union Station. (p145)

Venice Ale House Beers on a famous beach. (p130)

All Season Brewing Co Craft brews in a landmark former tire shop. (p102)

Best Old-School LA

No Vacancy Vintage Hollywood vibes and cocktails. (p49)

Dresden Lounge Legendary mid-century lounge captured in *Swingers*. (p62)

Polo Lounge The Beverly Hills Hotel's legendary bar. (p85)

Tiki-Ti Tiki classics in a tiny tropical bolthole. (pictured; p63)

Best Dive Bars

Frolic Room Anti-glam Hollywood dive that was frequented by Charles Bukowski. (p39)

Hinano Cafe Favored destination for boozers with sandy feet since 1962. (p131)

Top Bar Tips

○ Many bars require proof of age upon entry, no matter how old you look. Always take official photo ID.

○ Don't drink and drive. Under California law, the blood alcohol percentage is 0.08%.

Treasure Hunt

LA is a pro at luring cards out of wallets. After all, how can you not bag that supercute vintage-fabric dress? Or that tongue-in-cheek tote? And what about that mid-century-modern lamp, the one that perfectly illuminates that rare Hollywood film script you scored? Creativity and whimsy drive this town, right down to its wares.

Keep it Indie, Keep it Local

If you're into shopping with honor, and espouse a 'do no harm' lifestyle, then seek out LA's plethora of independent boutiques. You might find yourself scoring Cali-chic threads and handmade sneakers in Downtown's Arts District; rocker outfits, vintage and jars of artisan jam in Silver Lake and Echo Park; small-batch stationery and outrageous jumpsuits in Highland Park; or fair-trade beach bags in oceanside Venice. Museum shops are also often great for unique local gifts, from jewelry to ceramics.

Downtown Fashion District

Bargain hunters love the frantic 100-block warren in Downtown LA's Fashion District. Deals can be amazing, but first-timers are often bewildered by the district's size. For orientation, check out fashiondistrict.org.

Sample sales are usually held here on the last Friday of every month from 9am to 3pm.

Popular showrooms include the California Market Center, Cooper Design Space, Gerry Building and New Mart. Upcoming sales are posted on the LA Fashion District Instagram account (instagram.com/lafashiondistrict) and website (https://fashiondistrict.org/explore/calendar).

MSPHOTOGRAPHIC/SHUTTERSTOCK ©

Best Shopping Strips

Melrose Ave Style mavens of all ages. (p103)

Abbot Kinney Blvd Indie boutiques and international flagship stores. (pictured; p127)

Row DTLA Niche fashion, design and concept stores in a vast industrial complex. (p152)

Best for Local Design

Matrushka Fashion boutique loved by LA's creative types. (p65)

Shades of Grey Micah Cohen's progressive unisex fashion label. (p153)

Best Coastal Living

Aviator Nation Signature hoodies and casuals. (p132)

Bo Bridges Gallery Coastal art photography. (p135)

Best Offbeat

Wacko Warehouse of kitsch, with a welcome literary impulse. (p65)

Big Bud Press Retro-inspired jumpsuits, tees and more. (p74)

Best Pre-Loved Finds

Luxe De Ville Impeccably maintained and runway-worthy. (p65)

Lemon Frog Treasure trove of mid-century outfits and accessories. (p65)

It's a Wrap! Cast-offs from real TV shows and movies. (p167)

Amoeba Music Epic repository of vinyl, DVDs, CDs and collectables. (p53)

Best Bookshops

Last Bookstore An independent new and used giant in a former bank. (p153)

Skylight Books Community-minded bookstore with regular events. (p65)

Larry Edmunds Bookshop Original movie scripts and rare books on film and TV. (p53)

For Kids

Los Angeles offers a bounty of attractions and activities for young travelers, from theme parks to interactive museums to all those wonderful, sandy beaches. The pervasive casual style means that few restaurants are too stuffy for younger diners.

Best Districts for Kids

When it comes to engaging younger visitors, not all corners of LA were created equal. Top choices include Santa Monica, home to golden beaches, a much-loved bicycle trail and amusement rides on its eponymous pier, and the Cayton Children's Museum (cayton museum.org). More coastal fun awaits in neighboring Venice, its own assets including lots of cheap, weird stuff for sale along the boardwalk and a celebrated skatepark.

Further inland, Hollywood dazzles with its movie-industry landmarks, while Griffith Park offers everything from horseback-riding and hiking to zoo creatures, vintage trains and one of the world's finest planetariums. In Mid-City, the blocks of Wilshire Blvd directly east of Fairfax Ave are known as Museum Row due to the concentration of blockbuster cultural attractions, all within walking distance of each other.

North of Hollywood, the San Fernando Valley offers top-tier theme parks and movie-studio tours. South of LA, Orange County lures with the most magical kingdom of all, Disneyland.

Best Outdoor Fun

Disneyland® Resort World's most fabled theme park. (p170)

Universal Studios Hollywood Movie-themed thrills for young and old. (p160)

Griffith Park LA's attraction-packed communal backyard. (p60)

Santa Monica Pier Amusement rides and a fabulous beach. (pictured; p108)

Warner Bros Studio Tour Behind-the-scenes look

at a working movie studio. (p164)

Echo Park Lake Swan-shaped pedal boats and LA skyline views. (p67)

Best Rainy-Day Adventures

California Science Center Simulated earthquake and mind-expanding thrills. (p155)

Natural History Museum Millions of years explored through hands-on exhibits. (p155)

Griffith Observatory Grab a seat in the planetarium by day, peer into telescopes on the lawn by night. (p56)

Petersen Automotive Museum Complete with kids' section inspired by the movie *Cars*. (p98)

La Brea Tar Pits & Museum Child-friendly exhibits for future paleontologists. (p98)

Heal the Bay Aquarium Touch tanks crawling with crabs and crustaceans scooped from local waters. (p112)

Bob Baker Marionette Theater Shows draw from a cast of over 2000 puppets. (p71)

Best for Budding Creatives

Getty Center Hands-on creative fun, a kids' gift shop and play-friendly gardens. (p88)

Broad Pop paintings, a great kids' tour and the fantastical *Infinity Mirrored Room*. (p138)

Academy Museum of Motion Pictures Immersive journey through the world of movie making. (p92)

Best Kid-Friendly Eateries

Original Farmers Market Guaranteed to please the most finicky eaters. (p100)

Grand Central Market Colorful wonderland of affordable, casual bites. (p148)

Bob's Big Boy Fun, classic diner with spot-hitting burgers. (p164)

Salt & Straw Creatively flavored artisan ice cream. (p130)

Pink's Hot Dogs Always popular purveyor of tube steaks in myriad forms. (p101)

Responsible Travel

Positive, sustainable and feel-good experiences around the city.

Leave a Small Footprint

o Where possible, get from A to B using buses or Metro trains; the latter is a great way of avoiding LA's notorious traffic.

o Cycle; there is a growing network of bi-cycle trails across LA.

o Shop at LA's myriad vintage stores.

Walk LA's Neighborhoods

Los Angeles is dotted with walkable neigh-borhoods – there are more places to amble here than its car-centric reputation would suggest. The following are a few examples of areas where you can ditch the car and spend the day strolling.

Hollywood Hollywood Blvd is a carnival of sights.

Silver Lake & Los Feliz Vermont Ave, Hollywood Blvd and Sunset Blvd are lined with vintage shops, cafes and restaurants.

Echo Park Great and historic park and neighbor-hood.

Highland Park Figueroa St is a thriving strip.

West Hollywood Sunset Blvd is dotted with icons and surprises.

Beverly Hills Rodeo Dr and the surrounding blocks are a retail playland.

Mid-City Wilshire Blvd is lined with cultural power-houses; Melrose Blvd is the storied land of offbeat boutiques.

Santa Monica Downtown segues into the long pier and beaches.

Venice Walk the beach, canals and Abbot Kinney Blvd.

Downtown History, archi-tecture and classic movie backdrops.

Support Local

Visit farmers markets. Be wowed by the best local organic produce and food products. Top choices: the

RAW-FILMS/SHUTTERSTOCK ©

Hollywood Farmers' Market (p47) and the legendary Santa Monica Farmers Markets (p114).

Choose Sustainable Venues

Dine at ethical eateries. Eco-friendly practices are the norm at most LA eateries. One of the region's best restaurants, Hollywood's Providence, is a pioneer in using sustainable seafood. (p45)

Shop at ethical shops. Mid-City's Reformation prides itself on its use of

sustainable and vintage fabrics. (p103)

Bike the beaches. The fabulous Marvin Braude Bicycle Trail follows 22 miles of LA's best beaches. (pictured; p109)

Learn More

Museums bring the history of LA's incredibly diverse communities to life and offer histories that are often ignored.

Biddy Mason Memorial Park Celebrates an original Downtown property owner and philanthropist. (p146)

Japanese American National Museum Includes exhibits documenting the destruction and removal of LA's large population in WWII. (p145)

Museum of Social Justice Looks at local history through the filters of poverty, women's suffrage and civil rights. (p145)

California African American Museum Explores this huge community centered in South LA and beyond. (p155)

Museum of Tolerance Reflecting on light, darkness and the Holocaust. (p80)

Active LA

Despite spending a lot of time jammed on freeways, Angelenos love to get physical. Theirs is a city made for pace-quickening thrills, with spectacular mountain hikes and one of the country's largest urban nature reserves. Add to this almost 300 days of sunshine and you'll forgive the locals for looking so, so good.

ONEINCHPUNCH/SHUTTERSTOCK ©

Hiking

Los Angeles is hemmed in by two mountain ranges and countless canyons, serving up dramatic topography. Most remarkable is the sheer proximity of the city's hiking trails, and rugged mountain-lion country is within sight of Hollywood. Within LA, **Griffith Park** is one of the country's largest municipal parks, with over 50 miles of trails.

Skateboarding

In the 1970s, skateboarders on the Santa Monica–Venice border honed their craft by breaking into dry swimming pools in the backyards of homes (the 2005 film *Lords of Dogtown* chronicles their rise). Venice and its famous skatepark remain a hot spot for skaters and their fans. You can rent boards at Jay's Rentals (jaysrentalsvb.com) on the Boardwalk.

Best City Hikes

Runyon Canyon Short and relatively easy, with good celeb-spotting potential and city views. (p47)

Wisdom Tree, Cahuenga Peak & Mt Lee Summit Loop Spectacular, challenging and 4 miles long; with views of the city and mountains and a close-up look at the Hollywood sign. (p47)

Bronson Canyon An easy option leading to famous caves featured in retro TV hits *Batman* and *The Lone Ranger*. (p60)

Best on Wheels

Marvin Braude Bicycle Trail Catching a Pacific breeze on this celebrated 22-mile route. (p109)

Bikes & Hikes LA Tackling the 32-mile 'LA in a Day' cycling adventure. (p82)

Venice Skatepark Getting gnarly at LA's world-famous skateboarding mecca. (pictured; p123)

Live Music

The history of music in LA might as well be the history of American music, at least for the last eight decades. Much of the recording industry is based here, and the sheer abundance of world-class musicians, paired with spectacular and historic venues, make it a minor tragedy to leave town without a concert in the memory files.

EMMA_GRIFFITHS/SHUTTERSTOCK ©

Musical Choices

In your Los Angeles dream, you're a DJ – so what kind of music do you play? Beach Boys, West Coast rap, original punk, classic soul, hard bop, heavy metal, opera? Try all of the above. To hear the world's most eclectic playlist, just walk down an LA city street. From the electronic mixologists of Echo Park or the jazz cats of Blue Whale to the LA Phil or a legendary rock-and-roll band, the choice is yours. Download the Bandsintown app for listings.

Best Outdoor Venues

Hollywood Bowl LA's greatest gift to musicians and their fans. (p50)

Greek Theatre More intimate than the Bowl and almost as perfect. (pictured; p64)

Getty Center Free live acts and DJ sets during summer's Off the 405 series. (p88)

Best Indie Venues

El Rey Theatre Emerging and big-name acts in an art deco dance hall. (p102)

Echo + Echoplex Edgy mix of DJ-driven dance parties and new rockers. (p64)

Hotel Cafe Intimate venue known for booking rising acts. (p51)

Fonda Theatre Anything from singer-songwriters to synth-pop acts and new-school rappers. (p52)

Best Classical & Jazz Venues

Walt Disney Concert Hall World-class home of the LA Phil. (p144)

Dresden Lounge Old-school vibe with jazz performed most nights in Los Feliz. (p62)

Vibrato Grill Bar Designed by jazz legend Herb Alpert. (p85)

Beaches

With miles and miles of wide, sandy beaches, you'll find it hard to resist getting wet in LA. Beach life and surf culture are part of the free-wheeling SoCal lifestyle, so play hooky any day of the week and hit the waves like locals often do.

BILLION PHOTOS/SHUTTERSTOCK ©

Surf's Up! You Down?

Surfing tints every aspect of LA beach life, from clothing to lingo. The most powerful swells arrive in late fall and winter, while May and June are generally the flattest months, although they do bring warmer water. Speaking of temperature, without a wet suit, you'll likely freeze except at the height of summer. Shops in Santa Monica, Venice and elsewhere can provide gear and lessons.

Beach Volleyball

Beach volleyball originated in Santa Monica during the 1920s. You'll find nets up and down LA County's beaches, especially in Santa Monica, Venice and Manhattan Beach, where the **AVP Manhattan Beach Open** (Association of Volleyball Professionals; avp.com) happens every summer. Courts are open to the public; see beaches.lacounty.gov for details.

Best Beaches

Venice Boardwalk Sand, waves, street art and some of LA's best people-watching. (p122)

Santa Monica State Beach Best choice for families, with the famous pier and its rides close by. (p109)

Manhattan Beach Lots of space, lots of waves and a salubrious air. (p135)

South Venice Beach More sand, fewer people – and a pier. (p125)

El Matador State Beach Beachcomb on Malibu's most photogenic strip. (p169)

Celebrity Spotting

Admit it. You want to see a celeb. You're in Hollywood and LA, so don't apologize. Maybe it's the talent we love, or feeling connected to the world through one anointed person, or thinking we'll absorb a bit of that holy glow. Or maybe, just maybe, you can wrangle the selfie of selfies...

IVAN CHOLAKOV/SHUTTERSTOCK ©

Getting Your Star Fix

So where to look for stars? Restaurants are primo, especially in West Hollywood, Hollywood, Malibu, Los Feliz, Mid-City and, of course, Beverly Hills. Shopping works too, so browse A-list faves on Robertson Blvd, Melrose Ave and Abbot Kinney Blvd. Hillside trails are favored for working up a sweat.

Popular Celeb-Spotting Spots

Polo Lounge It's never *not* been the place to spot celebs. (p85)

Grandmaster Recorders Views of the Hollywood Hills and A-listers. (p46)

Craig's A Melrose Ave hideaway with a secluded back patio. (p84)

Mother Wolf Rollicking big-name hangout for Roman food in Hollywood. (p45)

Crossroads Kitchen Comfort food for the stars on the Sunset Strip. (p82)

Catch LA Rooftop eatery with paparazzi down below. (p82)

Fred Segal Top-shelf shopping yields top-shelf shoppers. (p86)

Live TV-Show Taping

You're pretty much guaranteed to see a star or two at a live TV-show taping. Apply for tickets well in advance online.

Under the Radar

WALTER CICCHETTI/SHUTTERSTOCK ©

From smoky market stalls peddling Latin bites to neighborly streets awash with indie-spirited coffee shops, bars and vintage stores, LA is richer than its celeb-centric image.

South LA

The massive area south of the I-10 Fwy comprises dozens of neighborhoods collectively called South LA. On its north end is Exposition Park. A couple of miles west, Leimert Park is the beating heart of LA's African American community, and east of the I-110 Fwy is Watts, known for **Watts Towers** (pictured; wattstowers.org), a masterpiece of folk art.

South LA is finally getting a new Metro light rail line, the K, which serves Leimert Park, Inglewood and other communities on its run to LAX. It boasts enormous displays of works by local artists.

Westlake

Once a glamorous enclave for silent-film stars, Westlake is now Downtown's raffish western neighbor, tempered by **MacArthur Park** (p99), the very one where 'someone left the cake out in the rain' in the eponymous Jimmy Webb song made famous by Donna Summer. Despite the whiff of gentrification, the neighborhood remains a gritty bastion of Hispanic *vida*.

One of its best-kept secrets is the **Guatemalan Night Market**, where throngs of *jornaleros* (day laborers) head nightly for cheap, authentic Latin American street food such as *longaniza* sausages, *garnachas* (fried corn tortillas topped with ground meat) and *hilachas* (stewed shredded beef with vegetables and rice). Bring cash.

EVGENY KARANDAEV/SHUTTERSTOCK ©

LGBTIQ+ Travelers

While your gaydar will be pinging throughout the county, the rainbow flag flies highest in Boystown, along Santa Monica Blvd in West Hollywood. Earthier scenes are found in Silver Lake and Downtown LA.

LGBTIQ+ Festivals

The festival season kicks off with LA Pride (lapride.org) in June, bringing huge crowds to West Hollywood (WeHo) for its exhibits, shows and parade down Santa Monica Blvd. It continues in August with Long Beach Pride (long beachpride.com).

May is also time for RuPaul's DragCon (https:// la.rupaulsdragcon. com), the world's largest drag-culture convention. Jump to Halloween (October 31) and around 500,000 outrageously costumed revelers of all persuasions hit Santa Monica Blvd for spectacular WeHo fun.

Best Performances

Celebration Theatre (celebrationtheatre.com) Ranks among the nation's leading companies for LGBTIQ+ plays.

Cavern Club Theater (cavernclubtheater.com) Drag shows and other fabulously kooky performances beneath a Silver Lake Mexican restaurant.

Gay Men's Chorus of Los Angeles (gmcla.org) This amazing group has been doing it since 1979.

Best Nightspots

The Abbey It's been called the best gay bar in the world. (p84)

Akbar Fun-loving, casbah-style spot for queer Eastsiders of all ages. (p63)

Honey's at Star Love Whimsical bar with karaoke. (p48)

Precinct Down-n-dirty, rock-and-roll-style bar Downtown. (p151)

Club Cobra Popular for drag and trans nights in the Valley. (p167)

Eagle LA As close as LA gets to a gay leather bar. (p63)

Four Perfect Days

Day 1

SEAN PAVONE/SHUTTERSTOCK ©

Walk all over your favorite stars on the **Hollywood Walk of Fame** (p38) and size up their handprints outside **TCL Chinese Theatre** (pictured; p39). For Hollywood history intrigues, hit the **Hollywood Museum** (p39).

Take a stroll on boutique-lined **Melrose Ave** (p103). If your idols are more Kubrick than Kardashian, snub the shops for the extraordinary **Academy Museum of Motion Pictures** (p92).

After dinner at historic old Hollywood **Musso & Frank Grill** (p44), laugh it up with live comedy at the **Laugh Factory** (p85) or **Improv** (p85).

Day 2

EDDIE HERNANDEZ.COM/SHUTTERSTOCK ©

Time to hit booming Downtown LA (DTLA), reserving tickets in advance to the spectacular modern art at **Broad** (p138), or explore the city's Hispanic roots at **El Pueblo de Los Ángeles Historical Monument** (p145).

Following lunch at **Grand Central Market** (pictured; p148), take in Broadway's heritage architecture before hitting high notes at the **Grammy Museum** (p144). Alternatively, shop stores in the Arts District and **Row DTLA** (p152) complex.

Have cocktails with a view at **Bar Clara** (p150), then dinner at **Orsa & Winston** (p149), where the Italian-Asian fare is some of LA's most inventive. Enjoy a performance at the **Los Angeles Music Center** (p152) or a basketball game at the **Crypto.com Arena** (p151).

Day 3

ESB PROFESSIONAL/SHUTTERSTOCK ©

Spend the morning at the **Getty Center** (p88), a spectacular synergy of art, architecture, landscaping and panoramic views. If possible, save your appetite for innovative, produce-driven **Gjusta** (p129) in ever-eclectic Venice.

Satiated, hunt down unique fashion, accessories and art along **Abbot Kinney Blvd** (p127), then stroll, pedal or Rollerblade along the **Venice Boardwalk** (p122), taking in its street art, nutty souvenirs and acres of powdery sand.

Wrap up the day in neighboring Santa Monica, catching another perfect SoCal sunset from **Santa Monica Pier** (pictured; p108) before a rooftop toast at **Penthouse** (p117) followed by dinner at **Cassia** (p114). Listen to blues at **Harvelle's** (p118).

Day 4

LARRY GIBSON/SHUTTERSTOCK ©

Roll things out with a **Warner Bros Studio Tour** (p164), visiting backlot sets and technical departments and eyeing up some of Hollywood's most famous movie props. If you prefer theme-park rides, opt for nearby **Universal Studios Hollywood** (p160).

Head up to the landmark **Griffith Observatory** (pictured; p56) in time to watch the sun sink over the city before an umbrella-topped drink at **Tiki-Ti** (p63) in Los Feliz. Have a dinner of iconic California cuisine at **All Time** (p61). Wrap up your adventure with jazzy tunes at mid-century **Dresden Lounge** (p62).

Need to Know

For detailed information, see Survival Guide (p177)

Language
English

Currency
US dollar ($)

Money
ATMs are widely available and card payment is accepted at most attractions and businesses. Contactless payments are preferred at many establishments.

Mobile Phones
5G service is found throughout Southern California. US prepaid rechargeable SIM cards are usually cheaper than using a non-US network.

Time
Pacific Standard Time (GMT/UTC minus eight hours).

Tipping
Tipping is *not* optional. See p184 for detailed tipping suggestions.

Daily Budget

Budget: less than $150
Dorm bed: $35–75
Takeout meal: $7–15
Free concerts and events
Metro daily fare cap: $5

Midrange: $150–300
Hotel double room: $200
Two-course dinner and glass of wine: $40
Live music concert: $50

Top end: more than $300
Beach or Downtown hotel: from $300
Dinner at a destination restaurant: from $80, excluding drinks

Advance Planning

Three months before Book accommodation and rental car, especially if visiting during busy festival or holiday periods.

One month before Reserve tickets to major performing arts and sporting events. Register for tickets to a live TV show production.

Two weeks before Reserve tickets to the Broad art museum, the Frederick R Weisman Art Foundation, any LA Conservancy walking tour, Disneyland and the Academy Museum of Motion Pictures. Reserve tables at top restaurants, particularly if dining later in the week.

Arriving in Los Angeles

Most travelers arrive in Los Angeles via air, although plenty of people also drive.

✈ From Los Angeles International Airport (LAX)

Around 35 to 60 minutes southwest of Downtown LA, subject to traffic.

Bus LAX FlyAway runs nonstop to Downtown (Union Station) and Van Nuys; times vary. Catch Big Blue Bus Line 3 or Rapid 3 to Venice and Santa Monica. Catch the shuttle to the Aviation/LAX station for the Metro C (Green) Line light rail.

Taxi/Rideshare Available 24 hours; around $60 to Downtown LA and Hollywood, around $35 to Venice and around $40 to Santa Monica (excluding tip).

Getting Around

Car culture still rules but LA's public transit options are improving.

🚇 Metro

Metro subway and light rail lines run from 4am or 5am to around 1am. Use a TAP card (bought in stations or online) for fares, which caps daily costs.

🚌 Bus

Metro buses run from 4am to 12:30am; some routes terminate earlier, some run all night. Fares from $1.75. Big Blue Buses operate from 5am or 6am to between 6pm and midnight. Fares from $1.25. DASH buses run from 6am or 7am (9am on weekends) to 5pm or 6:30pm. Fare $0.50.

🚕 Taxi

Taxis are expensive. On-demand car-service apps Uber and Lyft are at times cheaper.

BOB ROSSEROW / SHUTTERSTOCK ©

Los Angeles Neighborhoods

Burbank & Universal City (p159)
Home to a theme park, Sushi Row and most of LA's major movie studios. It's also the birthplace of car culture and porn.

West Hollywood & Beverly Hills (p77)
Big dollars and gay fabulous, wonderful shopping, sinful eateries and terrific nightlife, too. From here you can explore the entire city.

Universal Studios Hollywood ◉

Getty Center ◉

Academy Museum of Motion Pictures ◉ ◉

LACMA

Santa Monica (p107)
Mix with the surf rats, skate punks, yoga freaks, psychics and street performers along a stretch of sublime coastline.

← Malibu (5 miles)

Santa Monica Pier ◉

Venice Boardwalk ◉

Venice (p121)
Inhale an incense-scented whiff of Venice, a boho beach town and longtime haven for artists, New Agers and free spirits.

Miracle Mile & Mid-City (p91)
Museum Row is the big draw, but funky Fairfax and the old Farmers Market are worthy destinations.

Hollywood (p37)
The nexus of the global entertainment industry offers starry sidewalks, blingy nightclubs and celebrity sightings.

Highland Park (p69)
Booming northeast neighborhood with some of LA's coolest creative galleries, chic vintage stores and brand-new bars and eateries.

◉ *Griffith Observatory*

◉ *Hollywood Walk of Fame*

Griffith Park, Silver Lake & Los Feliz (p55)
Where hipsters and yuppies collide in an immense urban playground crowned with a window onto the universe.

◉ *Broad*

◉ *Exposition Park*

Downtown (p137)
Historical, multilayered and fascinating, it's become so cool that the likes of *GQ* have called it America's best downtown.

*Disneyland ®
Resort
(10 miles)*

Explore
Los Angeles

Hollywood **37**

Griffith Park, Silver Lake & Los Feliz **55**

Highland Park **69**

West Hollywood & Beverly Hills **77**

Miracle Mile & Mid-City **91**

Santa Monica **107**

Venice **121**

Downtown **137**

Burbank & Universal City **159**

Worth a Trip 🔭

Malibu 168

Disneyland® Resort 170

Los Angeles' Walking Tours 🥾

Cruising Echo Park 66

Culver City Shuffle 104

The Venice Stroll 124

Manhattan Beach, Sand and More 134

Ghosts of Downtown 140

Old & New in Pasadena 156

View of Los Angeles ONEINCHPUNCH/SHUTTERSTOCK ©

Explore
Hollywood

No other corner of LA is steeped in as much mythology as Hollywood. It's here that you'll find the Hollywood Walk of Fame, the Capitol Records Tower and TCL Chinese Theatre, where the hand- and footprints of entertainment deities are immortalized in concrete. Look beyond Hollywood Blvd and you'll discover a multifaceted neighborhood of swinging bistros, maverick galleries and villa-graced side streets littered with Old Hollywood lore.

The Short List

○ **Paramount Pictures (p42)** *Taking a tour of one of the world's most famous film studios.*

○ **Hollywood Museum (p39)** *Eyeing up Hollywood memorabilia in a former makeup studio for the stars.*

○ **Hollywood Bowl (p50)** *Catching an evening concert at LA's most iconic outdoor amphitheater.*

○ **TCL Chinese Theatre (p39)** *Comparing hand and shoe sizes with entertainment legends.*

○ **Musso & Frank Grill (p44)** *Sipping martinis at a dapper veteran of Hollywood's Golden Age.*

Getting There & Around

Ⓜ The B Line (Red) connects Hollywood Blvd to Los Feliz, Downtown LA and Universal Studios.

🚌 Metro Line 2 connects Sunset Blvd to West Hollywood and Westwood. Metro Line 4 connects Santa Monica Blvd to West Hollywood and Beverly Hills. Both bus lines reach Silver Lake, Echo Park and Downtown LA. The DASH Hollywood route runs a circuit around Hollywood.

Neighborhood Map on p40

Paramount Pictures (p42) 4KCLIPS/SHUTTERSTOCK ©

Top Experience

Go Star Spotting on the Hollywood Walk of Fame

Over 2600 performers have been honored with a pink-marble sidewalk star on Hollywood's Walk of Fame, its most famous stretch being Hollywood Blvd. Many of the neighborhood's main attractions gravitate around the intersection of Hollywood Blvd and Highland Ave, among them some genuine relics from Hollywood's Golden Age.

◉ MAP P40, G2

walkoffame.com

TCL Chinese Theatre

Ever wondered what it'd be like to stand in Tom Hanks' shoes? Just find his footprints among the many in the forecourt of this **world-famous movie palace** (tclchinesetheatres.com; 🏛). The exotic pagoda theater once known as Grauman's – complete with temple bells and stone heaven dogs from China – has shown movies since 1927 when Cecil B DeMille's *The King of Kings* first flickered across the screen.

Hollywood Museum

Something of Hollywood's attic, this musty **temple to the stars** (thehollywoodmuseum.com; 🏛) is a mishmash of movie and TV costumes, props and memorabilia chaotically spread across four floors. The museum is housed inside the Max Factor Building, which launched in 1935 as a glamorous beauty salon for Hollywood's leading ladies. Track down the toupees worn by Frank Sinatra and John Wayne and don't miss the 'Real to Reel' exhibit on LGBTIQ+ issues in the industry.

Dolby Theatre

The Academy Awards are handed out at the **Dolby Theatre** (dolbytheatre.com; Ⓟ), which has also hosted the American Idol finale, the ESPY Awards and the Daytime Emmy Awards. The venue is home to the annual PaleyFest, the country's premier TV festival, held in spring. Guided tours of the theater will have you sniffing around the auditorium, admiring a VIP room and catching the shine of an Oscar statuette.

★ Top Tips

○ New Walk of Fame stars are unveiled once or twice every month with the help of the celebrities themselves. See the website for updates.

○ Download free app Pride Explorer (thelavendereffect. org/tours) for an entertaining self-guided walking tour of Hollywood Blvd and surrounds.

✕ Take a Break

The dive bar **Frolic Room** (📞323-462-5890) is always ready for its close-up (eg *LA Confidential, Bosch*). Select a tune on the jukebox and get friendly with the barkeeps over supercheap drinks.

For a satisfying bite on the go, hit Joe's Pizza (p47) for authentic New York–style pie, offered whole or by the slice.

Hollywood

Hollywood

E
HOLLYWOOD HILLS
N Beachw
N Bronson Ave
N Orange Dr

F

G
N Orange Dr
Hollywood & Highland Mall
Hollywood/ Highland

H
Discover Los Angeles Visitor Information Center

1

Madame Tussaud's
7 ◉
33 ☆ Japan 6 ◉ House
M
3 ◉
ⓘ

Hollywood Blvd ◉
Hollywood Walk of Fame
☆ 36
TMZ Celebrity Tour

2

31 19
◉ ✕
Franklin Ave

Yucca St

Carlos Ave

| 0 | 100 m |
| 0 | 0.05 miles |

N Highland Ave

Hollywood/ Western
M
22 ◉
◉ 23

Hollywood Blvd

Carlton Way

N St Andrews Pl
N Serrano Ave
N Hobart Blvd
N Kingsley Dr

3

◉ 25

W Sunset Blvd
W Sunset Blvd

Hollywood Fwy

N Bronson Ave
N Van Ness Ave
N Western Ave

4

Fountain Ave
Fountain Ave

La Mirada Ave
Lexington Ave
N St Andrews Pl
Virginia Ave
27 ◉
Virginia Ave

Santa Monica Blvd

N Gower St
N Beachworth Dr
Gordon St
Tamarind Ave
N Van Ness Ave
N Ridgewood Pl
N Wilton Pl
N Western Ave

5

Beth Olam Memorial Park
2 Hollywood ◉ Forever Cemetery
Romaine St

Ⓝ | 0 | 500 m |
| 0 | 0.25 miles |

Paramount Pictures
◉ 1

For reviews see
◉ Top Experiences p38
◉ Sights p42
✕ Eating p44
◉ Drinking p47
☆ Entertainment p50
🔒 Shopping p53

6

Melrose Ave

E   F   G   H

Sights

Paramount Pictures

FILM LOCATION

1 ⊙ MAP P40, E6

Star Trek, Indiana Jones and the *Ironman* series are among the blockbusters that originated at Paramount, the country's second-oldest movie studio and the only major one still in Hollywood proper. Two-hour golf-cart tours of the studio complex are offered year-round, taking in the backlots and sound stages. Passionate, knowledgeable guides offering fascinating insights into the studio's history and the movie-making process in general. VIP tours include a meal but are not worth the much-higher fee. (paramount studiotour.com)

Hollywood Forever Cemetery

CEMETERY

2 ⊙ MAP P40, E5

Paradisiacal landscaping, vainglorious tombstones and epic mausoleums (plus a view of Paramount Studios over the wall) make for an appropriate resting place for some of Hollywood's most iconic dearly departed. Residents include Rudolph Valentino, Cecil B DeMille, Mel Blanc (his tombstone reads, 'That's all folks'), Jayne Mansfield, Judy Garland, punk rockers Johnny and Dee Dee Ramone, *Golden Girls* star Estelle Getty, Burt Reynolds and Anne Heche. (hollywoodforever.com; P ⫟)

TMZ Celebrity Tour

BUS

3 ⊙ MAP P40, H2

Cut the shame; we know you want to spot celebrities, glimpse their homes and laugh at their dirt. Superfun tours by open-sided bus run for two hours, and you may encounter some celebrities – even if it's just a Real Housewife C-lister. Tours depart from outside the Hard Rock Cafe. (tmz.com/tour; ⫟)

Real Los Angeles Tours

WALKING

4 ⊙ MAP P40, D2

Explore Hollywood on foot with these two-hour tours starting at the historic Pantages Theatre on Hollywood Blvd. Highlights include historic homes and sites connected to celebrities through the decades. You'll see how a small farming town turned into the frenetic tourist magnet of today. Excellent walking tours of downtown LA are also offered. (thereallosangelestours.com)

Whitley Heights

AREA

5 ⊙ MAP P40, B2

For a taste of Old Hollywood, wander the narrow streets of Whitley Heights, a residential preservation zone bordered by Franklin Ave to the south, Highland Ave to the west, and split in two by the 101 freeway to the north and east. Peppered with beautiful Moorish, Renaissance and Italianate-style villas, this was the city's first 'Beverly Hills.' Among the highlights are the Alto Nido Apartments (1851 N Ivar Ave), the location used for the initial home of the ill-fated Joe Gillis in *Sunset Boulevard*.

Japan House   CULTURAL CENTRE

6 MAP P40, G2

This gallery hosts changing exhibits of all things Japanese, from architecture to manga. Its sleek, non-lending library houses hundreds of titles on Japanese art, architecture, design, food and more. The library's adjoining 5th-floor terrace offers sweeping views of Hollywood and Downtown, while Japan House's culinary incubator hosts pop-ups featuring emerging chefs; check the website for special events. Sponsored by the Japanese government, it's tucked away by the Dolby Theatre. (japanhousela.com; P)

Madame Tussaud's   MUSEUM

7 MAP P40, F2

The better of Hollywood's two wax museums, this is the place to take selfies with motionless celebrities (Salma Hayek, Harry Styles and Angela Bassett), old-school icons (Charlie Chaplin, Marilyn Monroe, Clark Gable), movie characters such as Hugh Jackman's Wolverine from *X-Men,* chart-topping pop stars and all-time-great directors. (madametussauds.com;)

Capitol Records   LANDMARK

8 MAP P40, D2

You'll have no trouble recognizing this iconic 1956 tower, one of

Capitol Records

Hollywood Sights

Gallery Hopping

It's not all 'Lights, camera, action!' in Hollywood. Its list of assets also includes prolific commercial galleries specializing in modern and contemporary art. **Regen Projects** (Map p40, B5; regenprojects. com) hosts bold, edgy shows across all mediums, from photography, painting and video art to ambitious installations. It's well known for propelling the careers of some of Southern California's most successful and innovative artists, among them Matthew Barney, Andrea Zittel and Catherine Opie.

A short walk away, **Kohn Gallery** (Map p40, A4; kohngallery.com; P) also offers museum-standard exhibitions, with both heavyweights (Li Hei Di and Barbara Kruger) and emerging talent (Sophia Narrett and Octavio Abúndez) on its books.

LA's great mid-century buildings. Designed by Welton Becket, it resembles a stack of records topped by a stylus blinking out 'Hollywood' in Morse code. Some of music's biggest stars have recorded hits in the building's basement studios, including Nat King Cole, Frank Sinatra, the Beatles, Katy Perry and Sam Smith. Outside on the sidewalk, Garth Brooks and John Lennon have their stars.

Egyptian Theatre   LANDMARK

9 ⊙ MAP P40, B3

The Egyptian, the first of the grand movie palaces on Hollywood Blvd, premiered *Robin Hood* in 1922. The theater's lavish getup – complete with hieroglyphs and sphinx heads – dovetailed nicely with the craze a century ago for all things Egyptian. These days it's a shrine to serious cinema thanks to the nonprofit American Cinematheque and has enjoyed a lavish restoration thanks to Netflix, which is using it for premiers. (americancinematheque.com)

Eating

Musso & Frank Grill   AMERICAN $$$

10 ✖ MAP P40, B2

Hollywood history hangs in the thick air at Musso & Frank Grill, Tinseltown's oldest eatery (since 1919). Charlie Chaplin came here to knock back vodka gimlets, Raymond Chandler penned scripts in the high-backed booths, and movie deals were made on the old phone at the back. The menu favors old American classics like steaks and huge salads. It's in constant use as a shooting location; recent appearances include *Once Upon a Time in Hollywood* and *The Kominsky Method*. (mussoandfrank. com; P)

Mother Wolf ITALIAN $$$

11 MAP P40, C3

Superb Roman cuisine meets star power at this always bustling restaurant. The 1930s art deco building recalls Hollywood's glamour days while today's celebrities provide the sparkle. Owner Evan Funke has solid local chops that combine time at Spago with a family history of Oscars. Robust pastas, pizzas and superb desserts keep the crowds coming. (motherwolfla.com)

Petit Trois FRENCH $$$

12 MAP P40, B6

Good things come in small packages...like tiny, no-reservations Petit Trois! Owned by acclaimed TV chef Ludo Lefebvre (*Top Chef*), its two long counters are where fans squeeze in for smashing Gallic-inspired fare, from a wonderfully light Boursin-stuffed omelet to standout escargot and a cheese-oozing onion soup. It now has patio tables. (petittrois.com; P)

Providence SEAFOOD $$$

13 MAP P40, C6

A modern classic, chef Michael Cimarusti's James Beard Award–winning, two-Michelin-starred classic is known for turning superlative seafood into revelatory creations that never feel experimental for the sake of it. Flavors conspire in unexpected, memorable ways that are worth the hefty prices. The restaurant wins plaudits for its dedication to sustainable seafood. (providencela.com; P)

Musso & Frank Grill

Grandmaster Recorders

AUSTRALIAN $$$

14 🍽 MAP P40, C3

You may bump into an A-lister grabbing a smoke on the way into this buzzing bistro where Italian flavors are creatively accented with fresh flavors. The airy dining room was once home to the name-sake recording studio, but today the hits are made in the kitchen. Opt for a table up on the roof and you'll enjoy a Hollywood vista. (grandmasterrecorders.com)

Clark Street Diner

AMERICAN $$

15 🍽 MAP P40, D2

What looks like a humdrum motel coffee shop is actually a Holly-wood legend. Known by various names over the years, this low-key diner has not only appeared in movies like *Swingers,* it's also served as a haven for actors and writers nursing bottomless cups of coffee in between gigs. The menu looks familiar, but everything is flat-out boffo (oh, those blueberry pancakes!).

Trejo's Coffee & Donuts

BAKERY $

16 🍽 MAP P40, B5

In a town known for donuts, this corner shop stands out. Owned by actor Danny Trejo (*Heat*, *From Dusk Till Dawn*), the goods here reflect his Mexican heritage. Classic forms are given names and thematic flavors like the 'Abuelita,' which recalls lazy mornings at home with loved ones sipping hot chocolate. (trejosdonuts.com)

Hollywood Forever Cemetery (p42)

Luv2eat

THAI $

17 MAP P40, B3

Don't let the strip-mall location deter you, Luv2eat is a haven for Thai food, made all the more appealing by its location close to the Hollywood strip. Don't miss knockout choices such as Phuket-style crab curry, tangy *moo-ping* (grilled pork skewers) and the phenomenal papaya salad. (luv2eatthai.com; P🍷👪)

Joe's Pizza

PIZZA $

18 MAP P40, C3

Red-neon Joe's pumps out *proper* New York pizza by the slice. We're talking hand-tossed, pliable, thin crusts, with all the toppings. Parmesan and red pepper shakers are on standby for those who like it cheesy or hot, and there's a vegan-cheese pizza option for herbivores. Perfect for a quick, cheap bite on Hollywood Blvd. (joespizza.it; 👪)

Oaks Gourmet

DELI $

19 MAP P40, E2

This upscale deli and wine shop has a devoted following. Browse Californian vintages, specialty bottled cocktails, artisanal cheeses and other gourmet treats while waiting for your crowd-pleasing BLT (house bacon, tomato, avocado, brie and roasted shallot aioli on toasted sourdough). The breakfast burrito is a fave. (theoaksgourmet. com; P🛜👪)

Hollywood Hikes

Increase your daily steps with a hike or jog through **Runyon Canyon** (laparks.org/runyon). Its trails are highly popular with calorie-counting locals, including celebrities. (And you were wondering why one of the three main trails is called the Star Trail.) For a more challenging hike, tackle the spectacular **Wisdom Tree, Cahuenga Peak & Mt Lee Summit**, a rocky four-mile hilltop loop that leads to the back of the Hollywood Sign.

Hollywood Farmers' Market

MARKET $

20 MAP P40, D3

LA's largest farmers market is also one of its best, and its Sunday-morning sprawl offers organic and specialty produce from local farmers, producers and artisans. Some of the city's top chefs shop here, and you may spot the occasional celebrity. The market also offers tasty ready-to-eat bites and drinks. (seela.org/markets-hollywood; 👪)

Drinking

Javista Hollywood

COFFEE

21 MAP P40, B3

Tourists, industry stalwarts and those that defy easy categorization all get their morning breakfast

Dress Up or Dress Down?

Hollywood's bar scene is diverse and delicious, with a large number of venues on or just off Hollywood Blvd. You'll find everything from historic dive and cocktail bars, once frequented by Hollywood legends, to velvet-rope hot spots, buzzing rooftop hotel bars and even a rum-and-cigar hideaway. Some of the more fashionable spots have dress codes or reservations-only policies, among them La Descarga. Always check ahead.

drink fix at this neighborhood favorite just down from the Hollywood Museum. Drinks made with locally roasted coffee beans and a huge selection of teas pair with bagels, ubiquitous avocado toast and sandwiches. (javista coffee.com; 🛜)

Harvard & Stone BAR

22 🚇 MAP P40, H3

With daily rotating craft whiskey, bourbon and cocktail specials, Harvard & Stone lures partiers with its solid live bands, DJs and burlesque troops working their saucy magic. It's ski lodge meets steampunk factory, with a blues and rockabilly soul. Note the dress code, which discourages shorts,

shiny shirts, sports gear and flip-flops. (harvardandstone.com; 🛜)

Tabula Rasa Bar WINE BAR

23 🚇 MAP P40, H3

Thai Town's Tabula is everything one could want in a neighborhood wine bar: eclectic drops, unpretentious barkeeps, well-picked tunes and regular live gigs, including Sunday jazz. Offerings by the glass are short, sharp and engaging. Beers are equally intriguing and the Cuban sandwich and many small plates are all winners. (tabularasabar.com; 🛜)

Sassafras Saloon BAR

24 🚇 MAP P40, D4

You'll be pining for New Orleans at the moody Sassafras Saloon, which channels life on the bayou. Enjoy well-made Sazeracs and Vieux Carres plus live blues and DJ-spun tunes. It's open Friday and Saturday nights. (sassafras saloon.com; 🛜)

Honey's at Star Love LGBTIQ+

25 🚇 MAP P40, G3

One of Hollywood's most entertaining bars caters to an LGBTIQ+ crowd. The decor is whimsical and the drinks inventive, with many non-alcoholic options. Wednesday karaoke nights are legendary; other days the mood can be a bit mellower. (honeysla.com)

No Vacancy

BAR

26 MAP P40, C2

If you prefer your cocktail sessions with plenty of atmosphere, make a reservation online, style up and head over to this old shingled Victorian. It's a vintage Hollywood scene of dark timber panels and elegant banquettes, with bars tended by clever barkeeps while burlesque dancers and porch-playing musicians entertain the droves of party people. It's open Thursday to Saturday nights. (novacancyla.com; 🛜)

La Descarga

LOUNGE

27 MAP P40, G5

This reservations-only lounge offers more than 1060 types of rum from across the globe. The bartenders mix specialty cocktails, but you'd do well to order something aged and sip it neat as you enjoy live salsa and bachata tunes and, Thursday to Saturday, burlesque ballerinas. Book well ahead for Friday and Saturday. (ladescarga la.com)

Burgundy Room

BAR

28 MAP P40, C3

Old Hollywood rocks on at the historic Burgundy Room, a grungy former speakeasy with peeling bar stools, two super-snug booths and restrooms smothered in graffiti. You won't find seasonal cocktails here, just a timeless crowd of rockers, kicking back cheap (for Hollywood) drinks to blaring blues, indie and classic hard rock. (📞323-465-7530; 🛜)

Tabula Rasa Bar

Touring the Studios

Learn about how movies and TV shows are made on a tour of a working studio. Star-sighting potential is better than average, except during 'hiatus' (May to August) when studios are deserted.

Paramount Pictures (p42) One of Hollywood's oldest and classiest studios, the Paramount studios on Melrose cover 65 acres and have 30 sound stages. Among the movies shot here are *Sunset Boulevard* and *The Wolf of Wall Street*.

Sony Pictures (p105) The tour includes visits to the sound stages where *Men in Black*, *Spider-Man* and *The Wizard of Oz* were filmed. It was once the venerable MGM studio.

Warner Bros Studios (p164) This tour offers the most fun and authentic look behind the scenes. You'll see sound stages, famous backlots and technical departments, including props and costumes.

Bar Lis
LOUNGE

29 MAP P40, C3

All of Hollywood sweeps around you from this rooftop lounge on the 11th floor of the hip Thompson Hollywood. There's a bit of a posh Med vibe (Cannes anyone?) with plush seating and lush palms. Craft cocktails accompany lots of artful small plates. Later, tables are cleared and the dancing begins. (barlisla.com)

Entertainment

Hollywood Bowl
CONCERT VENUE

30 MAP P40, B1

Summers in LA just wouldn't be the same without alfresco melodies under the stars at the Bowl, a huge natural amphitheater in the Hollywood Hills. Its annual season – which usually runs from late May to September – includes symphonies, jazz bands and iconic acts such as Bob Dylan, Gladys Knight, Herbie Hancock and Boy George. Bring a sweater or blanket as nights get cool. (hollywoodbowl.com)

Upright Citizens Brigade Theatre
COMEDY

31 MAP P40, E2

Founded by *Saturday Night Live* alums Amy Poehler and Ian Roberts along with Matt Besser and Matt Walsh, this sketch-comedy group schedules numerous nightly acts. Shows span anything from stand-up comedy to improv to, yes, sketch. It's arguably the best comedy hub in town. (ucbcomedy.com)

Hotel Cafe

LIVE MUSIC

32 MAP P40, C3

Cheap cocktails and the chance of catching the next big act make this intimate, low-key music venue a big hit with insiders and celebrities. It's mainly a stepping stone for promising singer-songwriters and balladeers. Get there early and enter from the alley. (hotelcafe.com)

TCL Chinese Theatre

CINEMA

33 MAP P40, G2

Once inside past the tourist frenzy of the forecourt, this legendary cinema remains just that. Regularly used for film premiers, the main theater here retains its 1927 elegance and has a vast screen. It's one of the few cinemas in the world that can show 70mm film prints on an Imax screen, which is why director Christopher Nolan favored it for *Oppenheimer* screenings. (tclchinesetheatres.com)

Cinelounge Sunset

CINEMA

34 MAP P40, C3

Assigned seats, exceptional celeb-sighting potential and a varied program that covers mainstream and art-house movies make this complex a must. Bonuses: Q&As with directors, writers and actors. (cineloungefilm.com)

Hollywood Pantages Theatre

THEATER

35 MAP P40, D2

The splendidly restored Pantages Theatre is a 1930 art deco showplace from the Golden Age and

Hollywood Pantages Theatre

a fabulous place to catch a hot-ticket Broadway musical. It was the home of the Oscars through the 1950s. The no-nonsense exterior belies the lavish interior. (broadwayinhollywood.com)

El Capitan Theatre CINEMA

36 ⭐ MAP P40, G2

Disney rolls out family-friendly blockbusters at this movie palace, sometimes with costumed characters putting on the Ritz in live preshow routines. The best seats are on the balcony in the middle of the front row. It dates to 1926; *Citizen Kane* premiered here in 1941. (elcapitantheatre.com;)

Fonda Theatre CONCERT VENUE

37 ⭐ MAP P40, D3

Dating back to the Roaring Twenties, the since-restored Fonda Theatre remains one of Hollywood's best venues for live tunes. It's an intimate, (mostly) general-admission space with an open dance floor and balcony seating. Expect progressive acts, crooning vocalists and next-gen rappers. (fondatheatre.com)

Catalina Jazz Club JAZZ

38 ⭐ MAP P40, B3

It might be tucked in a ho-hum office building, but once you're inside this sultry jazz club all is forgiven. Expect a mix of top touring talent and emerging local acts – performers have included

El Capitan Theatre

Frank McComb, Monty Alexander, Barbara Morrison, Kaylene Peoples and Marcus Miller. One or two shows nightly, best reserved ahead. (catalinajazzclub.com)

Shopping

Amoeba Music   MUSIC

39 🔒 MAP P40, D3

When a record store not only survives but thrives in the streaming age, you know it's doing something right. Flip through 500,000 new and used CDs, DVDs, videos and vinyl at this cult-status music hub, which also stocks band-themed T-shirts, music memorabilia, books and comics. (amoeba.com)

Counterpoint   MUSIC, BOOKS

Woodblock stacks are packed high with used fiction here at Counterpoint (see 31 ⭐ Map p40, E2), while plywood bins are stuffed with vinyl soul, classical and jazz. Ask to see the hidden back rooms, home to the real (albeit pricier) gems. Staff recommendations show off their encyclopedic knowledge and diverse tastes. (counterpointla.com)

Larry Edmunds Bookshop   BOOKS

40 🔒 MAP P40, B3

For decades this cluttered old-school shop has been the place to go for all types of entertainment industry books, new and used. You can find out-of-print bios of long-dead celebs mixed with classic tomes on acting and scriptwriting techniques. Browse the bins of lobby cards for classic films. (larry edmunds.com)

JF Chen   DESIGN

41 🔒 MAP P40, A5

A go-to for professional curators, celebrities and their interior decorators, JF Chen offers two cluttered floors of museum-quality furniture and decorative arts from greats such as Poul Kjærholm, Ettore Sottsass, and Charles and Ray Eames. There's never a shortage of extraordinary pieces. (jfchen.com)

Explore

Griffith Park, Silver Lake & Los Feliz

Pimped with stencil art, inked skin and skinny jeans, Silver Lake is a vibrant enclave, home to buzzing eateries and well-curated boutiques. Just west, easy-living Los Feliz harbors screenwriters, low-key celebrities and some legendary bars. North of Los Feliz lie the canyons and trails of Griffith Park, home of the famous Griffith Observatory.

The Short List

○ **Griffith Observatory (p56)** *Scanning LA and the galaxy from a world-famous landmark.*

○ **Hiking the Hills (p60)** *Escaping the rat race.*

○ **Hot Spot Dining (p60)** *Taste-testing the area's dynamic food scene.*

○ **Retail Adventures (p65)** *Picking up unique wares on Sunset Blvd.*

○ **Dresden Lounge (p62)** *Catching jazz in a gracious Old Hollywood setting.*

Getting There & Around

🚃 Metro Lines 2 and 4 run along Sunset Blvd; Line 2 buses then head south on Alvarado St. Line 2 reaches Hollywood, West Hollywood and Westwood. Line 4 reaches Downtown, Hollywood, West Hollywood and Beverly Hills. All reach Echo Park.

Ⓜ The B Line (Red) connects to Hollywood, Universal Studios and Downtown LA. Vermont/Santa Monica station lies 0.7 miles west of Sunset Junction in Silver Lake. Alight at Vermont/Sunset station for Los Feliz.

Neighborhood Map on p58

Griffith Park (p60) HANNATOR/SHUTTERSTOCK ©

Top Experience 📷

Discover the Stars at Griffith Observatory

LA's landmark 1935 observatory opens a window onto the universe from its perch on the southern slopes of Mt Hollywood. It also offers a prime view of the 50ft-tall, sheet-metal Hollywood Sign, an LA icon that first appeared in the hills in 1923 as an advertising gimmick for a real-estate development called 'Hollywoodland.'

◉ MAP P58, B3

www.griffithobservatory. org

P 👤

Samuel Oschin Planetarium

The observatory's planetarium is one of the world's finest, with a state-of-the-art Zeiss star projector, digital projection system and high-tech aluminum dome that transforms into a giant screen that feels impressively realistic. Three daily shows are offered: *Centered in the Universe* takes visitors back to the Big Bang, *Signs of Life* will have you searching for life in the solar system, while *Water Is Life* explains why planetary research looks for water.

Leonard Nimoy Event Horizon Theater

The observatory's lower levels were added during an ambitious restoration, which included lifting the entire building off its foundations. Insight is offered in a 24-minute documentary screened in the Leonard Nimoy Event Horizon Theater and narrated by the late *Star Trek* actor himself. It also sheds light on the observatory's founder, Griffith J Griffith but avoids mention of the more problematic aspects of his life.

Telescopes, Views & Jimmy Dean

The rooftop viewing platform offers boffo views of LA and the Hollywood Hills. Visitors are welcome to peer into the Zeiss Telescope on the east side of the roof; after dark, staff wheel additional telescopes out to the front lawn for star gazing. LA's hulking deco observatory is no stranger to the spotlight itself, having made cameos in numerous movies and TV shows, among them *La La Land, Terminator, 24* and *Alias*. The film it's most associated with, however, remains *Rebel Without a Cause*, commemorated with a bust of James Dean on the west side of the observatory lawn.

★ Top Tips

○ Head up on a clear day to make the most of the spectacular views of the entire LA Basin, surrounding mountains and Pacific Ocean.

○ If you're driving and only heading up for the views, do so on a weekday before noon (when the observatory opens) for easier parking.

○ During opening hours, parking can be a trial, especially on weekends. Take the DASH Observatory/Los Feliz shuttle bus from Vermont/Sunset metro station or hike up from Los Feliz below.

✗ Take a Break

While there's a nondescript cafe at the observatory, a better option is to follow the signposted 0.6-mile hike down to Fern Dell Dr for freshly baked goods and sandwiches at outdoor, counter-service cafe **Trails** (☏323-871-2102; 📶♿).

Griffith Park, Silver Lake & Los Feliz

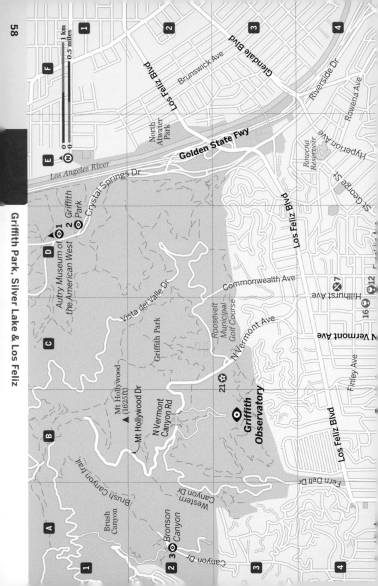

0 — 1 km
0 — 0.5 miles

Brunswick Ave

Los Feliz Blvd

Glendale Blvd

Riverside Dr

Rowena Ave

North
Atwater
Park

Golden State Fwy

Hyperion Ave

Los Angeles River

Crystal Springs Dr

Rowena
Reservoir

St George St

Autry Museum of
the American West

Griffith
Park

Los Feliz Blvd

Commonwealth Ave

Hillhurst Ave

Vista del Valle Dr

Roosevelt
Municipal
Golf Course

N Vermont Ave

N Vermont Ave

Finley Ave

Griffith Park

Mt Hollywood
▲ (1625ft)

N Vermont Canyon Rd

Mt Hollywood Dr

Griffith
Observatory

Los Feliz Blvd

Brush Canyon trail

Fern Dell Dr

Brush
Canyon

Bronson
Canyon

Western Canyon Dr

Canyon Dr

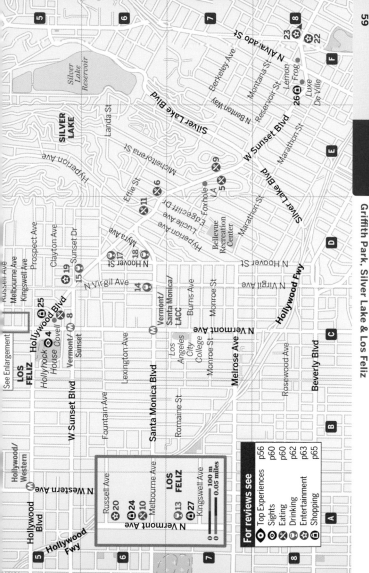

Griffith Park, Silver Lake & Los Feliz

SILVER LAKE

LOS FELIZ

Silver Lake Reservoir

Silver Lake Blvd

W Sunset Blvd

Silver Lake Blvd

N Alvarado St

N Benton Way

Berkeley Ave

Montana St

Reservoir St

Marathon St

Lemon
Frog
Luxe
De Ville

Hyperion Ave

Landa St

Micheltorena St

Effie St

Lucile Ave
Edgecliff Dr
Foxhole
LA

Bellevue Recreation Center

Marathon St

Hollywood Fwy

Clayton Ave

Prospect Ave

Sunset Dr

Myra Ave

N Hoover St

N Virgil Ave

N Hoover St

N Virgil Ave

Hyperion Ave

Russell Ave
Melbourne Ave
Kingswell Ave

Hollyhock House
Vermont/ Sunset

W Sunset Blvd

Fountain Ave

Lexington Ave

Santa Monica Blvd

Los Angeles City College

Vermont/ Santa Monica/ LACC

Burns Ave

Monroe St

N Vermont Ave

Melrose Ave

Monroe St

Romaine St

Rosewood Ave

Beverly Blvd

Hollywood/ Western

N Western Ave

Hollywood Blvd

Hollywood Fwy

See Enlargement

LOS FELIZ

Hollywood Blvd

Russell Ave

Melbourne Ave

Kingswell Ave

N Vermont Ave

LOS FELIZ

0   100 m
0   0.05 miles

For reviews see
Top Experiences   p56
Sights   p60
Eating   p60
Drinking   p62
Entertainment   p63
Shopping   p65

Sights

Autry Museum of the American West

MUSEUM

1 🎯 MAP P58, D1

Established by singing cowboy Gene Autry, this expansive, under-rated museum offers contemporary perspectives on the history and people of the American West, as well as their links to today's culture. Permanent exhibitions span Native American traditions to 19th-century cattle drives, daily frontier life (look for the beautifully carved vintage saloon bar) to costumes and artifacts from Hollywood westerns. (theautry.org; P♿)

Griffith Park

PARK

2 🎯 MAP P58, D1

Five times the size of New York's Central Park and home to the Griffith Observatory (p56), Greek Theatre (p64) and Autry Museum, LA's communal backyard covers more than 4300 acres of land, with over 50 miles of hiking trails. It's where you'll find the **LA Zoo** (lazoo. org; P♿) and the quaint train museum **Travel Town** (traveltown. org; P♿).

Gifted to the city in 1896 by mining mogul Griffith J Griffith, the park is considered a rare example of unspoiled chaparral. Access is easiest via the Griffith Park Dr or Zoo Dr exits off I-5 (Golden State Fwy). (laparks.org/griffithpark; P♿)

Bronson Canyon

HIKING

3 🎯 MAP P58, A2

Although many people prefer to do their running, walking and hiking in Runyon Canyon, we prefer Bronson. A wide fire road rises to a lookout point and links to the Hollywood sign, Griffith Park and the famed **Bronson Caves** – where scenes from the old *Batman* TV series and countless movies such as the 1956 *Invasion of the Body Snatchers* were shot. (laparks.org/park/bronson-canyon)

Hollyhock House

ARCHITECTURE

4 🎯 MAP P58, C5

Oil heir Aline Barnsdall commissioned Frank Lloyd Wright to design this hilltop arts complex and residence in 1919. With its central courtyard, porches and pergolas, the home is seen as a transitory moment in the architect's style, which evolved into a more open-plan, indoor–outdoor style that would help define modern Southern Californian living. It's been designated a Unesco World Heritage Site. The surrounding Barnsdall Park has grand views. (https://barnsdall.org/hollyhock-house; P)

Eating

All Day Baby

DINER $$

5 🍴 MAP P58, E7

Brilliant diner that merges American and Asian comfort food. Breakfasts lean more traditional with fare like biscuits, but as the day progresses the menu branches out to include fabulous flavors from around the Pacific. The banana cream pie is divine. (alldaybabyla.com)

Pine & Crane
TAIWANESE $$

6 MAP P58, E6

You'll be licking your chopsticks at this popular fast-casual spot for Taiwanese-inspired small plates, noodles and rice-based dishes. Feast on spicy shrimp wontons, nutty *dan dan* noodles and the unmissable beef roll, a burrito-like concoction packed with tender beef and piquant hoisin sauce. (pineandcrane.com;)

All Time
CALIFORNIAN $$

7 MAP P58, D4

All Time celebrates California produce and flavors. Breakfast or lunch, tuck into breakfast sandwiches or French toast with proper maple syrup. Dinner features a short, market-driven menu featuring seasonal fare. Lots of veggie options. (alltimelosangeles. com;)

HomeState
TEX-MEX $

8 MAP P58, C5

Texan transplant Briana Valdez is behind this tasty ode to the Lone Star State, where locals queue patiently for authentic breakfast tacos and rustic Texan creations such as a brisket sandwich made

Hollyhock House

with Mexican flair. Lots of shady outdoor seating. (myhomestate.com)

Playita Mariscos   MEXICAN $

9 🍴 MAP P58, E7

Homemade tortillas and fresh seafood star at this simple and simply wonderful Mexican cafe that recalls the owner's trips to the beach as a child. You won't have a hard time choosing: the menu consists of tacos, dorados, quesadillas and ceviche – and that's it. The authentic flavors extend to the cabbage (used instead of lettuce). Plenty of seating outside. (playitamariscos.com)

Figaro Bistrot   FRENCH $$

10 🍴 MAP P58, A6

A culinary ménage à trois involving a boulangerie, bistro and lounge, Figaro channels Paris with its heavy framed mirrors, sidewalk tables with authentic wicker chairs and Gallic-inspired fare. Baked goods include perfect croissants. The coffee crowd slowly morphs into a drinking crowd, just like any proper cafe in the City of Light. (figarobistrot.com)

Pazzo Gelato   GELATO $

11 🍴 MAP P58, D6

Florence-style gelato in LA. If it's fresh at local farmers markets, it's likely a flavor here. The seasonal fresh peach gelato is worth setting a calendar alert for; year-round flavors are luscious and good.

Appealing cafes and shops are nearby. (pazzogelato.net)

Drinking

Maru Coffee   COFFEE

12 ☕ MAP P58, D4

In a mellow, Korean-accented minimalist space of timber and concrete, Maru brews superb specialty coffee made with house-roasted beans. Other offerings include beautiful teas and matcha lattes. Stop here before hitting Griffith Park. (marucoffee.com; 📶)

Dresden Lounge   COCKTAIL BAR

13 ☕ MAP P58, A7

Old-school lounge where the drinks are served by staff in a timeless style. Expect proper martinis, smooth G&Ts and the knowledge to craft any other choice from the cocktail back bench. On Wednesday through Friday nights, jazzy combos provide entertainment. (thedresden.com)

Virgil   BAR

14 ☕ MAP P58, D6

A vintage-inspired hangout with creative cocktails and a stocked calendar of top-notch comedy, live music, disco and DJs. Highlights include an eclectic lineup of generally irreverent stand-up comics. Other rotating events include poetry slams, sketch acts and techno events. Reserve ahead for table service. (thevirgil.com)

Specialty Drinking Dens

Oenophiles will find their happy place at Los Feliz bar **Covell** (Map p58, C5; barcovell.com), its 150 wines by the glass showcasing interesting vineyards and lesser-known regions. Snug sake bar **Ototo** (ototo. la) pours a rotating selection of Japanese rice wines and serves up snacks just like you'd find in a back-alley drinking den in Tokyo.

Tiki-Ti   BAR

 15 🏠 MAP P58, D5

Channeling Waikiki since 1961, this tiny tropical tavern packs in everyone from stylish slummers to 'non-ironic' partiers in Hawaiian shirts. Drinks are strong and smooth; order the tequila-fueled Blood and Sand and expect a ritual that involves raucous cheers of 'Toro.' Most drinks are served in comically themed collectibles. (tiki-ti.com)

Big Bar   BAR

16 🏠 MAP P58, C4

The bar LA's top bartenders hang out at when they're off work. The drinks list is long, creative and intriguing, and guest bartenders craft their favorites. Inside it's intimate and dark; the outdoor back patio is low-key and relaxed. (instagram.com/bigbaralcove/)

Akbar   LGBTIQ+

17 🏠 MAP P58, D6

Fun-loving, casbah-style Akbar is a hit with queer Eastsiders of all ages. It's diverse, attitude-free and a refreshing antidote to the look-at-me WeHo scene. There's no shortage of themed nights, from live acts and karaoke to late-week dance sessions with renowned DJs. There's a jukebox to boot. (akbarsilverlake.com)

Eagle LA   GAY

18 🏠 MAP P58, D6

The walls are black, the lights are red and the videos are hardcore; the Eagle is as close as LA gets to a proper gay leather bar. It's also a friendly neighborhood hangout, with a pool table and a mixed crowd reveling in the indoor-outdoor space. (eaglela.com; 📶)

Entertainment

Vista Theatre   CINEMA

19 ⭐ MAP P58, D5

Dating back to 1923, the single-screen Vista is fresh off a 100-year anniversary revamp of its wonderfully kitsch 'ancient Egyptian' interior. The current owner is none other than Quentin Tarantino, who promises an eclectic lineup of first-run and classic films. The director promises that many will be projected from 35mm or 70mm film as opposed to digital. There's a good cafe with outdoor seating. (vintagecinemas.com/vista)

Los Feliz Theatre   CINEMA

20 ⭐ MAP P58, A6

A gem of a neighborhood cinema, this 100-year-old triplex screens first-run movies. The American Cinematheque chooses a good mix of classics and arthouse films. (vintagecinemas.com/losfeliz)

Greek Theatre   LIVE MUSIC

21 ⭐ MAP P58, C3

The 'Greek' in the 2010 film *Get Him to the Greek* is this 5900-capacity outdoor amphitheater, tucked into a woodsy Griffith Park hillside. A more intimate version of the Hollywood Bowl, it's much

loved for its vibe and variety – recent acts include George Lopez, Van Morrison, Regina Spektor and Dominic Fike. (lagreektheatre.com)

Echo + Echoplex   LIVE MUSIC

22 ⭐ MAP P58, F8

Eastsiders pack this crowded dive, basically a sweaty bar with a stage and a back patio. Known for punk rock, other styles here include in-die, electronica, dub reggae, dream and power pop. Monday nights are the domain of up-and-coming house bands. (theecho.com)

Dodger Stadium   BASEBALL

23 ⭐ MAP P58, F8

Few teams can match the Dodgers' history (Jackie Robinson, Sandy Koufax, Kirk Gibson and sports-

Dodger Stadium

caster Vin Scully), success and fan loyalty, and this mid-century stadium east of Echo Park (built on what was once the vibrant Mexican American neighborhood of Chavez Ravine) is still considered one of baseball's most scenic, framed by views of palm trees and the San Gabriel Mountains. Buy tickets ahead, games sell out. (mlb.com/dodgers/ballpark; 🏟)

Shopping

Skylight Books   BOOKS

24 🔒 MAP P58, A6

This much-loved Los Feliz institution carries everything from art, architecture and fashion tomes to LA history titles, vegan cookbooks, queer literature and critical theory. There's a solid selection of niche magazines and local zines, some great lit-themed tees and regular, engaging in-store readings and talks (with the podcasts available on the store's website). Great staff picks. (skylightbooks.com)

Wacko   COLLECTIBLES

25 🔒 MAP P58, C5

Billy Shire's sprawling carnival of pop, kitsch and camp has been a fun browse for decades. Pick up a Ziggy Stardust T-shirt, a *Star Wars* tote or perhaps a latex unicorn mask. You'll find a great selection of comics and books, including works by noted LA authors. The 'Build your own conspiracy' kit is a top seller. (soapplant.com)

Shopping VintageVille

Silver Lake and neighboring Echo Park are home to a string of renowned vintage stores. Standouts include **Luxe de Ville** (Map p58, F8; 📞213-353-0135), with its curated collection of rare frocks; **Lemon Frog** (Map p58, F8; 📞213-413-2143; lemonfrogshop.com), which has affordable duds from the '60s to the '90s; and **Foxhole LA** (Map p58, E7; foxholela.com), which deals in T-shirts and denim.

Matrushka   FASHION & ACCESSORIES

26 🔒 MAP P58, F8

Writers, film-industry types and independent style queens love Matrushka, a boutique and workshop owned and run by designer Lara Howe. The frocks, jumpsuits, leggings and more are all made in LA using bold, vintage-inspired fabrics. The pieces are affordable and accommodate all sizes. (matrushka.com)

Kingswell   SPORTS & OUTDOORS

27 🔒 MAP P58, A7

One of LA's best skateboard shops has gear and its own line of clothing. The staff are all skateboarders and share a wealth of info with visitors. The building has a notable history: the brothers Walt and Roy Disney opened their first animation studio here in 1923. (kingswell.tv)

Walking Tour 🥾

Cruising Echo Park

Plunge into a classic LA interface of urban art, music, vintage shops and hipster culture in the multiethnic neighborhoods in Echo Park. The landmark lake and fountain are looking spiffy after a revamp; happily, the panaderías and cevicherías remain amid the gentrification.

Walk Facts

Start Eightfold Coffee;
🚉 Metro Line 4

Finish Angels Point,
🚉 Metro Line 4

Length 4 miles; four hours

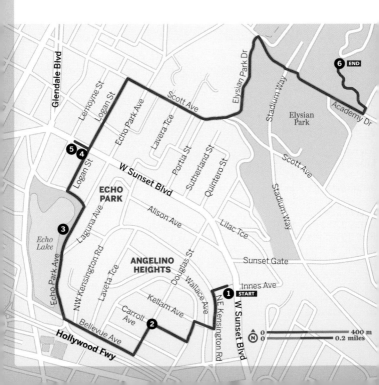

❶ Joe & Jewels

Eastside stylists and musicians flock to minimalist, whitewashed **Eightfold Coffee** (eightfoldcoffee. square.site; 📶) to talk gigs and sip superlative joe. Order one to go and check out the imaginative artisan jewelry at neighboring Esqueleto.

❷ Painted Ladies

Stairs beside Esqueleto lead up to Angelino Heights, established in the mid-1880s as one of LA's first suburbs. Its most charming street is **Carroll Ave**, home to the largest concentration of (mostly restored) Victorian-era homes in the city. Number 1345 appears in Michael Jackson's *Thriller* music video, while number 1329 was Halliwell Manor in the TV series *Charmed*.

❸ Echo Park Lake

A former reservoir, **Echo Park Lake** (laparks.org/aquatic/lake/ echo-park-lake; 🅿 ♿) is best known as the setting for Jake Gittes' surreptitious rowboating shenanigans in *Chinatown*, and for its keyhole vistas of the Downtown skyline. Find the boathouse amid the lush gardens and rent a swan-shaped pedal boat.

❹ Brews & Tacos

If you're hungry, slip into **Sage** (sageveganbistro.com; 📶 ♿ ♿), a scrumptious vegan kitchen that uses produce from its own farm and brews its own kombucha and beer. It's got outdoor tables, too. Or, across the street, the El Ruso food truck serves succulent tacos made with smoky beef ribs, which featured on Netflix's *Taco Chronicles*.

❺ Lakeside Reads

Wander through a mini maze of new and used literature inside **Stories** (storiesla.com; 📶), where the offerings include interesting LA-themed books. Score anything and everything from plays, poetry and short-story anthologies to graphic novels and brain-twisting metaphysics titles. Brainy types congregate in the back-end cafe, which comes with free wi-fi and a cute back patio.

❻ Hilly Views

Head up Logan St, turn east on Scott Ave and enter the vast green expanse that is Elysian Park. Follow the paths uphill to **Angels Point**. Under towering public art, you'll enjoy relatively unknown views of LA, including Dodger Stadium, Downtown and Hollywood.

Explore
Highland Park

Highland Park is happening. Its walkable, low-rise streets have been transformed into an in-the-know hub of restored Craftsman homes, Insta-worthy coffee shops, restaurants, bars and shops, all living side by side with throwback taquerias, barbers and Mexican grocery stores. This is not a place to tick off big-ticket sights. It is, however, the perfect place to absorb East LA at its coolest, grassroots best.

The Short List

○ **Retail Surprises (p73)** *Scoring locally made stationery, fashion and vinyl while on a great stroll.*

○ **Villa's Tacos (p71)** *Feasting on some of LA's best tacos.*

○ **Kumquat Coffee Co (p72)** *Eavesdropping on creatives over superlative joe.*

○ **Highland Park Bowl (p71)** *Striking out at a steampunk-inspired bowling-alley bar.*

○ **Los Angeles Police Museum (p71)** *Getting the dirt on LA crime from serial killers to famous robbers.*

Getting There & Around

Ⓜ The A Line (Blue) connects Highland Park to Downtown LA and Pasadena. Highland Park station lies one block behind the main drag, N Figueroa St.

🚌 Metro Line 182 runs along N Figueroa St and York Blvd.

Neighborhood Map on p70

Kumquat Coffee Co (p72) JIM_BROWN_PHOTOGRAPHY/SHUTTERSTOCK ©

Highland Park

N Figueroa St

York Blvd

N Figueroa St

Arroyo Seco Pkwy

110

HIGHLAND
PARK

Branch St

Meridian St

Los Angeles
Police
Museum ◉1

Roy St

Aldama St

Mesa Ave

Outlook Ave

N Figueroa St

Highland
Park

4

HIGHLAND
PARK

S Avenue 60

8 10
6

Hayes Ave

Fayette St

N Ave 61

N Ave 60

N Ave 59

S Avenue 58

N Ave 65

Highland
Park M

S Avenue 57

Nolden St

N Ave 56

York Blvd

◉14

Buchanan St

Baltimore St

Aldama St

Hub St

N Ave 57

Highland
Park
Bowl 2

7

S Avenue 5

11

N Ave 55

N Ave 56

N Ave 56

13

12

16

N Figueroa St

3

Stratford Rd

N Ave 54

N Ave 54

Ash St

Monte Vista St

Marmion Way

N Ave 55

N Ave 53

Irvington Pl

Holland Ave

Aldama St

Bob Baker
Marionette
Theater 18

Scoops

Donut
Friend

5

N Ave 52

N Ave 51

9

15 17

Buchanan St

Baltimore St

N Avenue 50

N Avenue 50

Lincoln Ave

York Blvd

Armadale Ave

8

El Paso Dr

Tce 49

Cleland Ave

0.5 miles

1 km

For reviews see	
◉ Sights	p71
✕ Eating	p71
◑ Drinking	p72
◐ Shopping	p73

Sights

Los Angeles Police Museum
MUSEUM

1 ◉ MAP P70, F2

Crime fighting is in the spotlight at Police Station No 11 (1926), now repurposed as a museum. Exhibits trace the history of the LAPD, from its humble beginnings in 1869 to the modern force of today. There's fascinating background on some of the city's most notorious crimes, but don't expect much on the more controversial aspects of the department. (laphs.org; P ⛹)

Highland Park Bowl
BOWLING

2 ◉ MAP P70, D4

You'll be hard-pressed to find a bowling alley as stunningly original as this one, its steampunk fit-out including upcycled pinsetters-turned-chandeliers, leather Chesterfield sofas and twin bars serving rotating craft cocktails and beers. (highlandparkbowl.com)

Eating

Villa's Tacos
MEXICAN $

3 🍴 MAP P70, D4

Tucked into the corner of a strip mall, Villa's serves up award-winning Mexican fare. Order the Villas Trio, a combo plate of three tacos made with blue-corn tortillas that combine veggie, chorizo and pork options. The salsa bar is

Top Billing for Puppets

A former vaudeville theater is home to the much-loved **Bob Baker Marionette Theater** (Map p70, B1; bobbaker marionettetheater.com; ⛹), LA's oldest children's theater company. The cast includes over 2000 puppets, some from the 1940s.

sublime, in particular the mango habanero.

Mariscos El Faro
MEXICAN $

4 🍴 MAP P70, F3

Make a beeline to this popular lunchtime food truck for the *empanadas de camaron*: a tortilla stuffed with cheese, shrimp and onions and then deep-fried until crispy. The rest of the menu focuses on top-notch seafood tacos and tostadas. Take your plate to the adjoining Highland Park for a picnic. (ordermariscoselfaro.com)

Joy
TAIWANESE $

5 🍴 MAP P70, C1

This casual eatery whips up Taiwanese-inspired brilliance in a flash. Snap at plump wontons, flavor-packed *mapo* tofu and crunchy thousand-layer pancakes, best jacked up with chili sauce, basil, cheese and egg. The scallion bread sandwiches are also worth a bite. (joyonyork.com; 🖊 ⛹)

Kitchen Mouse   VEGETARIAN $

6 MAP P70, E4

Adorned with freshly picked flowers and sidewalk tables, homey Kitchen Mouse is Highland Park's favorite herbivore. People flock here for generous, mood-lifting vegan and vegetarian dishes, especially the avocado TLT: a blissful combo of avocado, maple-tempeh bacon, cherry tomatoes and Dijon aioli. Good coffee, too. (kitchenmousela.com;)

Cafe Birdie   MODERN AMERICAN $$

7 MAP P70, E4

Market-fresh ingredients drive elevated comfort dishes at this slinky Highland Park hot spot, complete with the requisite marble-topped bar and an intimate, light-strung back patio. Birdie's pasta dishes and creative cocktails are gorgeous. (cafebirdiela.com;)

Queen St Raw Bar & Grill   SEAFOOD $$$

8 MAP P70, A1

Platters of raw oysters and grilled fish and octopus stream from the kitchen at this hugely popular bistro, whose vibe comes courtesy of the old waterfront in Charleston, SC. Grab a seat at the marble-topped horseshoe bar or reserve one of the tables outside on a quiet plaza. (queenstla.com)

Drinking

Kumquat Coffee Co   COFFEE

9 MAP P70, B1

This welcoming, minimalist space brews consistently superb coffee with meticulous attention to detail and local and international roasts. More unusual options include a popular *hojicha* (green tea) latte; pastries are from Highland Park's excellent Mr Holmes Bakehouse. (kumquatcoffee.com;)

La Cuevita   BAR

10 MAP P70, E4

The large patio at this mellow bar is the perfect spot to enjoy taco Tuesday happy hours. In keeping with the Mexican theme, the wall behind the bar is lined with bottles of tequila and mezcal. There's jazz on Sundays. (lacuevitabar.com)

ETA   COCKTAIL BAR

11 MAP P70, E4

One of the city's top cocktail dens, intimate ETA serves innovative, complex libations – try the surprising Lawler's Law. Happy hour brings trays of raw oysters on ice; the mural art is courtesy of local artist Johnny Tarajosu. (etahlp.com)

Gold Line   BAR

12 MAP P70, D4

Vinyl is king at mellow hi-fi bar Gold Line (the local Metro line before it became the A Line). Its hefty record collection (over 8000) lines the walls and includes rare discs from bar co-founder, DJ and music producer Peanut Butter Wolf. Let the good vibes flow over superb drinks. (goldlinebar.com; 🛜)

Shopping

On Maritime Records   MUSIC

13 MAP P70, D4

As shipshape and clean-lined as a racing yacht, this used record store has a wonderfully curated

Highland Park Shopping

Los Angeles Police Museum (p71)

selection of vinyl. Staff love to share recommendations. Known for rare finds and good prices. (onmaritimerecords.square.site)

Galco's Old World Grocery   FOOD & DRINKS

14 🔒 MAP P70, E2

You'll find over 700 small-batch and heritage sodas at this family-run grocery store, from botanically brewed British cola to legacy brands such as Frostie blue cream soda. You can even make your own using flavors such as toasted marshmallow and huckleberry. Heighten the sugar rush with some old-school candy – gotta love the Necco wafers! (sodapopstop.com)

Big Bud Press   FASHION & ACCESSORIES

15 🔒 MAP P70, B1

At the end of the rainbow lies this explosion of Technicolor grooviness. Designed and made in LA, its size-inclusive, unisex booty includes '70s-inspired jumpsuits in juicy hues, retro striped tees and outrageous power suits that would make Marcia Brady squeal. High-profile collaborators have included Lisa Hanawalt of the animated series *BoJack Horseman*. (bigbud press.com)

Avalon Vintage   VINTAGE

16 🔒 MAP P70, D4

One of the best-loved consignment stores in LA, Avalon is known

Galco's Old World Grocery

for stocking unusual retro frocks, gowns and outfits. You'll also find an eclectic and deep collection of old vinyl records, with offerings including classic rock and pop, soul, jazz and reggae. (avalon-vintage. business.site)

Shorthand STATIONERY

17 MAP P70, B1

Shorthand carries adorable cards and stationery, including items made by in-house letterpress printer Iron Curtain Press. There's a range of pens, pencils and other design-savvy desk essentials, as well as popular graphic-themed prints of LA and California. Bonus finds: amusing pins, embroidered patches and locally made soy-wax candles. (https://shopshorthand.com)

Dotter CONCEPT STORE

18 MAP P70, B1

Launched by a mother-daughter team, this artfully curated boutique has a more grown-up

Heart of Hispanic Culture

South of Highland Park and due east of Downtown in Boyle Heights is the traditional heart of Hispanic culture in LA. A good place to start is **Mariachi Plaza**. Mexican mariachi musicians dressed in their traditional charro suits have been descending on the old-school *zócalo* (public square) since the 1930s, trolling for work. Competing for attention is the entrance to Mariachi Plaza metro station, with its colored-glass main canopy evocative of a Mexican folk dancer's fan.

feel than many of its neighbors. Women and children are the main focus, which means anything from chic tunics, linen overalls and leather boots to handmade jewelry, adorable baby outfits and quality toys. (dotterstore.com;)

Explore ◈

West Hollywood & Beverly Hills

LA rainbows end in West Hollywood (WeHo), an independent city with way more punch and unbridled revelry than its 1.9-sq-mile frame might suggest. Packed with famous comedy clubs, legendary showbiz hotels and trendy, celeb-frequented restaurants and boutiques, it's also the city's gay heartland. To the west is salubrious Beverly Hills, home to high-end shopping strip Rodeo Drive and swanky bistros filled with power-lunching entertainment execs.

The Short List

○ **Comedy (p85)** *Laughing at the artistry of comics from yesterday, today and tomorrow at famous clubs.*

○ **Polo Lounge (p85)** *Gin martinis and Hollywood anecdotes at Beverly Hills' most famous drinking hole.*

○ **Museum of Tolerance (p80)** *Reflecting on light, darkness and the Holocaust.*

○ **Abbey (p84)** *Starting (and ending) here on a rainbow-colored bar crawl of Boystown.*

○ **Bikes & Hikes LA (p82)** *Getting LA-fit on a 32-mile sightseeing ride.*

Getting There & Around

🚌 Metro Line 2 connects Sunset Blvd in West Hollywood to Westwood, Hollywood, Silver Lake, Echo Park and Downtown LA. Metro Line 4 runs frequently along Santa Monica Blvd in West Hollywood and Beverly Hills, also reaching Hollywood, Silver Lake, Echo Park and Downtown LA.

Neighborhood Map on p78

West Hollywood & Beverly Hills

For reviews see

⊙ Sights   p80
✕ Eating   p82
🍷 Drinking   p85
★ Entertainment   p85
🔒 Shopping   p86

Greystone Mansion & Gardens: The Doheny Estate
⊙ 4

Coldwater Canyon Dr

Schuyler Rd

N Doheny Dr

Doheny Rd

Doheny Rd

Loma Vista Dr

W Sunset Blvd

Cynthia St

Lexington Rd

W Sunset Blvd

Elevado Ave

Lomitas Ave

N Sierra Dr
N Alta Dr
N Arden Dr
N Hillcrest Rd
N Palm Dr
N Maple Dr
N Elm Dr
Foothill Rd
N Alpine Dr
Carmelita Ave
N Rexford Dr
N Crescent Dr
N Canon Dr

Santa Monica Blvd

14 🍷

Frederick R Weisman Art Foundation
1 ⊙
4 ★ 17

Beverly Gardens Park

Foothill Rd
N Elm Dr
N Maple Dr
N Palm Dr
N Doheny Dr

N Beverly Dr

N Rodeo Dr
N Camden Dr
N Bedford Dr
N Roxbury Dr
N Linden Dr
Walden Dr

W 3rd St

Burton Way

Union 76 Gas Station
Dayton Way

Beverly Hills Visitors Center ℹ
✕ 12

N Canon Dr

BEVERLY HILLS

Clifton Way

S Wetherly Dr

Santa Monica Blvd

Rodeo Drive

N Beverly Dr

✕ 10

Wilshire Blvd

Wilshire Blvd

Charleville Blvd

N Rodeo Dr

S Beverly Dr

2 ⊙ Museum of Tolerance

E   F   G   H

Chateau
Marmont
5

Laugh
Factory

W Sunset Blvd   1

Comedy
Store

William
S Hart
Park

Fountain Ave

WEST
HOLLYWOOD   2

Norton Ave

N Crescent Heights Blvd

SUNSET
STRIP

9
W Sunset Blvd

18

19

Holloway Dr
Visit West
Hollywood

21 22

Santa Monica Blvd

N Flores St

Romaine St

Willoughby St

N Kings Rd

N Sweetzer Ave

N Laurel Ave

N Edinburgh Ave

N Hayworth Ave

N Fairfax Ave

WEST
HOLLYWOOD
13

6
Bikes &
Hikes LA

Waring Ave

3
Schindler
House

3

Trunks
Micky's
Saint
Felix

The
Abbey

Pacific
Design
Center

West Knoll Dr

N La Cienega Blvd

20

Melrose Ave
8

Improv

7
Melrose Ave

11

15

N San Vicente Blvd

Huntley Dr

BEVERLY
CENTER
DISTRICT

Clinton St

Rosewood Ave

N Fairfax Ave

4

N Robertson Blvd

16

Oakwood Ave

Alden Dr

Beverly Blvd

W 1st St

S Edinburgh Ave

The
Grove

5

W 3rd St
Burton Way

Colgate Ave

N Hamel Dr

S Sherbourne Dr

S Corning St

S San Vicente Blvd

S Orlando Ave

S Sweetzer Ave

W 3rd St

Colgate Ave

S La Jolla Ave

S Fairfax Ave

S Swall Dr

Wilshire Blvd

Charleville Blvd

6

E   F   G   H

0   1 km
0   0.5 miles

West Hollywood & Beverly Hills

Sights

Frederick R Weisman Art Foundation
MUSEUM

1 MAP P78, A4

The late entrepreneur and philanthropist Frederick R Weisman had an insatiable passion for art, a fact confirmed when touring his former Holmby Hills home. From floor to ceiling, the mansion (and its manicured grounds) bursts with extraordinary works from visionaries such as Picasso, Kandinsky, Miró, Magritte, Rothko, Warhol, Rauschenberg and Ruscha. Reserve tours in advance.

The mansion itself was designed by architect Gordon Bernie Kaufmann, whose projects include the Hoover Dam.

Check the website for special exhibitions held off-site. (weisman foundation.org)

Museum of Tolerance
MUSEUM

2 MAP P78, C6

Run by the Simon Wiesenthal Center, this deeply moving museum uses interactive technology to engage visitors in discussion and contemplation of the timeless scourges of racism and bigotry. Particular focus is given to the Holocaust, with a large exhibition that examines the events and the experiences of the millions who were persecuted. A companion exhibition offers an intimate look into the life and impact of Anne Frank. *Para Todos Los Niños* (Fighting Segregation in California) details

Pacific Design Center

KIT LEONG/SHUTTERSTOCK ©

Architectural Landmarks

West Hollywood, Beverly Hills and neighboring Century City claim numerous important architectural landmarks. Argentinian architect César Pelli (designer of Kuala Lumpur's Petronas Towers) is the mastermind behind the **Pacific Design Center** (PDC; Map p78, E3; pacificdesigncenter.com). Built in stages between 1975 and 2013, its three glass buildings – in red, green and blue – resemble giant, geometric toys. Further west, the **Union 76 Gas Station** (Map p78, C5) is a fine example of Googie architecture, a mid-century SoCal style informed by the era's burgeoning space industry and car culture. Built in 1965, its acclaimed architect Gin Wong had originally envisaged it as part of his LAX airport masterplan.

discrimination against Latinos in Southern California.

The museum's goal is for visitors – largely groups of schoolchildren – to learn and absorb the hard lessons of the past so they aren't repeated. Diversity is discussed, intolerances that we all carry are exposed, and champions of rights in America are celebrated. Among the museum's many fascinating artifacts are original diary entries written by Anne Frank as well as a copy of the so-called Gemlich letter, believed to be the first record of Hitler's anti-Semitic beliefs. (The original letter is safely archived at the Simon Wiesenthal Center across the street.) (museumoftolerance.com; P 🚻)

Schindler House   ARCHITECTURE

3 ◎ MAP P78, G3

The former home and studio of Vienna-born architect Rudolph Schindler (1887–1953) offers a fine

primer on the modernist elements that so greatly influenced mid-century California architecture. The open floor plan, flat roof and glass sliding doors, all considered avant-garde back in the 1920s, became design staples after WWII. (makcenter.org)

Greystone Mansion & Gardens: The Doheny Estate   NOTABLE BUILDING

4 ◎ MAP P78, C2

Featured in countless movies and TV shows (The Big Lebowski, There Will Be Blood), this 1927 Tudor Revival mansion was designed by Hoover Dam architect Gordon Bernie Kaufmann. It was a gift from oil tycoon Edward L Doheny to his son Ned and his family. In 1929 the oil heir and his male secretary were both found dead in an alleged murder-suicide – a mystery that has been debated endlessly ever since.

Beverly Hills Experience

Superb walking tours of Rodeo Drive and celebrity homes are easily followed in the free **Beverly Hills Experience app** (beverlyhillshistorical society.org) from the Beverly Hills Historical Society. The routes are clearly marked and as you walk you'll find one fascinating tidbit after another. The home tour leads you around a classic, palm-shaded section of BH where you'll see houses used by Frank Sinatra, Barbra Streisand, Eddie Murphy, Lucille Ball, George Clooney and many others.

While the elegant grounds – which offer commanding views of LA – are open daily, the lavish interior is only open sporadically. (beverlyhills.org/greystone; P)

Chateau Marmont
NOTABLE BUILDING

5 ◎ MAP P78, G1

Looming over the Sunset Strip, this storied hotel mixes Gothic details with a mishmash of French Loire Valley chateau inspiration. It's a fabled place, used by celebrities for close to 100 years – a tradition that continues today. Romances have started and ended here. Lives have ended here, too. Look for the discreet door in the wall that leads to the bungalow

where John Belushi died. In the 1970s, rockers regularly tossed TVs out of the windows. You can get a feel for the vibe in the bestselling 2023 thriller *Everybody Knows*. (chateaumarmont.com)

Bikes & Hikes LA
OUTDOORS

6 ◎ MAP P78, F2

This WeHo-based outfit rents bikes and offers cycling tours of LA, Hollywood and Beverly Hills, as well as the signature 32-mile 'LA in a Day' taking in celebrity homes, swank shopping streets, inspiring architecture and the Pacific. Excellent hiking tours venture around Griffith Park and the Hollywood Sign. (bikesandhikesla.com; 🚹)

Eating

Catch LA
FUSION $$$

7 🍴 MAP P78, E4

You may well find sidewalk paparazzi stalking celebrity guests, but such distractions are forgotten once you saunter into this 3rd-floor rooftop restaurant and bar. Graze on East-West, surf-centric share plates. Solid if not groundbreaking, with an optional vegan menu, excellent cocktails and fabulous people-watching. (http://catch restaurants.com/catchla; P 📶 ♿)

Crossroads Kitchen
VEGAN $$

8 🍴 MAP P78, G3

Tal Ronnen didn't become a celebrity chef (*Oprah, Ellen*) by serving ordinary vegan fare. Instead, he focuses on seasonal creations made from surprising and delicious combinations of ingredients, alongside pizzas and pastas incorporating innovative 'cheeses' made from nuts. Dining here is an event where everyone is honored, whether you're an A-lister or not. (crossroadskitchen.com; P 🖊)

Butcher, the Baker, the Cappuccino Maker
AMERICAN $$

9 🍴 MAP P78, E2

Literally and spiritually at the heart of the Sunset Strip, bright, airy indoor-outdoor BBCM does Insta-ready comfort food: eggs Benedict, bananas Foster French toast, braised short ribs, halibut fish and chips and sushi burritos. Cakes and pastries look like museum pieces. It's the perfect lunch pause while prowling the strip. (bbcmcafe.com)

Spago
CALIFORNIAN $$$

10 🍴 MAP P78, C6

Wolfgang Puck's empire started here and this is where his heart remains. Most evenings Puck still turns up to work the dining room of his foundational restaurant, where California flavors are celebrated with the changing seasons. After 30 years the cooking remains fresh and inventive, the service polished and gracious, and the diners rested and happy. (wolfgangpuck.com/dining/spago)

Bungalow, Chateau Marmont

WeHo, Follow the Rainbow

West Hollywood is one of the world's top spots for gay nightlife, with dozens of shops, restaurants and nightspots along Santa Monica Blvd – the highest concentration is in between Robertson Blvd and Palm Dr. **The Abbey** (Map p78, E3; theabbeyweho.com; 🔊) has been called the world's best gay bar, with a multitude of polished indoor-outdoor spaces. **Saint Felix** (Map p78, E3; https://saintfelix.net; 🔊) is great for happy hour, lacking the overdrive feel of some of its neighbors. **Micky's** (Map p78, E3; mickys.com; 🔊) is a quintessential WeHo dance club, with go-go boys and lots of beautiful people. The crowd skews somewhat older at **Trunks** (Map p78, E3; west.hollywood.trunksbar.com; 🔊), a low-lit brick-house dive that's more down to earth.

Craig's   AMERICAN $$$

11 🍽 MAP P78, E4

Upscale comfort food is served in a relaxed dining room, on the back patio or out on the front

The Abbey

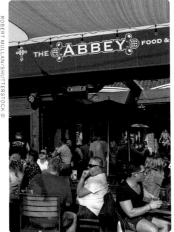

ROBERT MULLAN/SHUTTERSTOCK ©

porch. Gas-powered heaters keep diners warm as they dig into seemingly plebeian choices (mac and cheese) under vine-draped arbors. It's the patrons that really shine here, as Craig's is the place to go for A-listers who want something familiar and rib-sticking. (craigs.la)

Nate'n Al's   DELI $$

12 🍽 MAP P78, B5

When this old-school Jewish deli announced it was closing in 2018, movie moguls across Beverly Hills teamed up and helped to get it a sequel. Today, it once again has the most appealing sidewalk tables close to Rodeo Dr and the kitchen continues to prepare superb versions of the deli classics. Pro tip: it serves booze. (natenals.com)

Tail O' the Pup

HOT DOGS $

13 MAP P78, F3

You can't miss the big weenie in the bun – it's right beside the road – and you can't miss with anything on the menu at this casual West Hollywood icon. Hot dogs are served in a variety of ways (the 'jalapeno pup' will perk you right up) and there are also burgers, corndogs, fries and even grilled cheese. Shady tables, too. (tailothepup.com)

Drinking

Polo Lounge

COCKTAIL BAR

14 MAP P78, A4

For a classic LA experience, dress up and swill evening martinis in the Beverly Hills Hotel's legendary bar. Charlie Chaplin had a standing lunch reservation at booth 1. Movies still matter here, and studio titans really do hammer out deals at the tables while top celebs ponder strategies with their agents. (dorchestercollection.com/en/los -angeles/the-beverly-hills-hotel; 📶)

EP & LP

ROOFTOP BAR

15 MAP P78, F3

Scan the Hollywood Hills for the house that *you* would live in, while you sip excellent cocktails at one of LA's largest and most popular rooftop bars. Pick a table under a palm tree and savor the views from Beverly Hills to Downtown. On many nights, the Melrose Roof-top Theatre screens classics and recent hits. (eplosangeles.com)

Entertainment

Largo at the Coronet

COMEDY

16 ⭐ MAP P78, F4

Largo is an incubator of high-minded pop culture (it nurtured Zach Galifianakis to stardom). Part of the Coronet Theatre complex, it features edgy comedy as well as nourishing night music from the likes of resident singer-songwriter Jon Brion. (largo-la.com)

Vibrato Grill Bar

JAZZ

17 ⭐ MAP P78, A4

You can thank jazz legend Herb Alpert for the standout acoustics

---

Laugh Riot

Some of America's top comics got their chops at WeHo's comedy clubs. The **Comedy Store** (Map p78, F1; thecomedy store.com; 📶) has been a thing since it brought in hot young comics such as Robin Williams and David Letterman. The Marx Brothers kept offices at the **Laugh Factory** (Map p78, H1; laughfactory.com) and it still gets big names. **The Groundlings** (p103) present superb sketch comedy, while the **Improv** (Map p78, G3; improv.com) draws big names like Maz Jobrani, Nikki Glazer and Jay Mohr.

here. After all, he designed the elegant, romantic spot. A restaurant and jazz club in one, it serves up six nights of stellar acts. Reservations (and dressy outfits) are highly recommended. (vibratogrill jazz.com)

Whisky-a-Go-Go　　LIVE MUSIC

18 ⭐ **MAP P78, E2**

Like other Sunset Strip venues, the Whisky trades heavily on its legend status. This was where the Doors were the house band and go-go dancing was invented back in the '60s. Still, making the rounds between here and nearby fabled music venues like the Viper Room and the Roxy Theatre is an elemental Sunset Strip experience. (https://whiskyagogo.com)

Shopping

Fred Segal　　FASHION & ACCESSORIES

19 🔒 **MAP P78, F2**

No LA shopping trip is complete without a stop at Fred's. This is its flagship store, 21,000-sq-ft of chic, Cali-casual threads, accessories, beauty products and homewares hip enough for cashed-up celebs. The space also hosts regular product drops, trunk shows and live music. (fredsegal.com)

Gucci Salon Melrose　　CLOTHING

20 🔒 **MAP P78, F3**

Inside this ivy-covered temple of high fashion, you can always hear a pin drop. Which is good, as fittings

Whisky-a-Go-Go

Shop for Ultra-Luxe on Rodeo Drive

If you fancy the ultra-luxe lifestyle, then click your Jimmy Choos together for a trip to **Rodeo Dr** (Map p78, B6; rodeodrive-bh.com), a three-block ribbon of consumption that features every major luxury brand on the planet. It's pricey and unapologetically pretentious, but hey, you're in Beverly Hills. Fashion retailer Fred Hayman opened the strip's first boutique – Giorgio Beverly Hills – at number 273 back in 1961. And like the dowagers at a Chanel No 5 giveaway, the number soon proliferated.

Architecturally, nothing is especially noteworthy – even the Frank Lloyd Wright–designed shops at number 328 are ho-hum. Rather, the success of a day here is measured by the number of glossy brand-name shopping bags you can load onto your arms. Don't expect to see any celebrities, however. The top brands all have private shopping areas for the rich and famous, so they need not mix with the hoi polloi.

for custom creations like gowns, suits and shoes are an ongoing affair. Gucci's premier store requires a reservation to enter. Once inside, it's the glossiest pages of fashion magazines and runway shows come to life. (gucci.com)

Mystery Pier Books BOOKS

21 🔒 MAP P78, E2

Famed for stocking signed shooting scripts from blockbusters, Mystery Pier also sells rare and obscure 1st-edition books, from Shakespeare and Salinger to JK Rowling. Amid the treasures is a curated selection of mystery and detective fiction. (mysterypierbooks.com)

Book Soup BOOKS

22 🔒 MAP P78, E2

This shop is overflowing with over 60,000 titles, including entertainment, travel, feminist and queer studies, not to mention eclectic, edgy and LA-based fiction. There's a great selection of magazines. Regular in-store author events feature big names. (booksoup.com)

Top Experience

Admire the Art and Architecture of the Getty Center

Straddling a hilltop in the Santa Monica Mountains, the palatial Getty Center offers an irresistible feast of art, design and botanical beauty. Ponder the myths and landscapes of Dossi, Van Gogh and Cézanne, gaze out over the City of Angels and kick back in a verdant wonderland of gurgling water, lush lawns and world-famous sculptures.

getty.edu

P

Collections

The Getty's collections focus on European art, with a concentration on works from the 19th and 20th centuries. There are genuine treasures here. In the east pavilion, seek out Gentileschi's *Danaë and the Shower of Gold* and Rembrandt's self-portrait *Rembrandt Laughing*. In the west pavilion, look for Van Gogh's *Irises*, Monet's *Wheatstacks, Snow Effect, Morning*, Manet's *Jeanne (Spring)* and Turner's *Modern Rome – Campo Vaccino*. The south pavilion's outdoor terrace is home to Marino Marini's excitable bronze *Angel of the Citadel*, originally owned by Hollywood producer Ray Stark of *Steel Magnolias* fame, while the grounds themselves are studded with prized sculptures, including three works by Henry Moore.

Architecture & Gardens

As famous for its form as it is for its art, the Getty Center originates from the drawing board of Pritzker Prize–winning architect Richard Meier. Completed in 1997 at a cost of $1.3 billion, the complex is clad in 16,000 tons of cleft-cut travertine sourced from the same Italian quarry used to construct Rome's ancient Colosseum. Look closely and you'll spot fossilized shells, fish and foliage.

Events

Aside from free tours throughout the day, there are also a wide range of mostly free events, including talks, symposia and curated film screenings. Some require reservations, though standby tickets are often available. On Saturday evenings from May to September, the center hosts **Off the 405**, a popular series featuring top progressive pop and world-music acts in the Getty courtyard.

★ Top Tips

◦ Visit early morning or mid-afternoon. Sunsets create a remarkable alchemy of light and shadow and are especially magical in winter. Saturday nights are usually not too crowded and parking is $15 after 3pm.

◦ Check the website in advance and stop by the info desk to find out about all the day's tours and special events. Download the essential GettyGuide app.

◦ Free and worthy audio guides are available in the lobby. Bring a photo ID.

✕ Take a Break

The Getty Center is home to a fine-dining, modern American restaurant and two casual cafes. While all three are fine and offer outdoor seating, none are outstanding. Consider bringing a picnic lunch to enjoy on the grounds.

Explore ◈

Miracle Mile & Mid-City

Mid-City may not have the flirtatious rep of West Hollywood to the north, nor the fabled glamour of Beverly Hills to the west, but these gridded streets claim some of LA's top cultural and retail assets. It's here that you'll find the 'Miracle Mile' and its string of blockbuster museums, the Orthodox Jewish-meets-hipster Fairfax district and world-famous Melrose Ave, as much a bastion of pop culture as it is a bustling shopping strip.

The Short List

○ **Academy Museum of Motion Pictures (p92)** *Celebrating cinema at an Oscar-worthy film museum.*

○ **LACMA (p94)** *Diving into an eclectic feast of top-tier artworks.*

○ **Petersen Automotive Museum (p98)** *Purring over Hollywood-famous wheels.*

○ **Melrose Avenue (p103)** *Shop hopping and celebrity spotting on a cult-status strip.*

○ **Groundlings (p103)** *Splitting your sides at the improv school that spawned Kristen Wiig and Pee Wee Herman.*

Getting There & Around

🚌 Metro Line 10 runs along Melrose Ave, Metro Line 14 serves Beverly Blvd and both Metro Lines 212 and 217 connect the two thoroughfares to Wilshire Blvd further south.

Neighborhood Map on p96

Petersen Automotive Museum (p98)

Top Experience

Learn Everything about Film at the Academy Museum of Motion Pictures

Channel your inner movie-lover at LA's lavish film museum. Spectacular and expansive, it's a cutting-edge ode to motion arts and sciences, with thought-provoking exhibits, priceless memorabilia and a dynamic program of screenings and talks delving deep into celluloid culture. If you only have time for one museum, make it this one.

◉ MAP P96, D5

academymuseum.org

Exhibitions

Kick off with a visual overview of cinema's evolution in the Spielberg Family Gallery before tackling the core Stories of Cinema galleries on the second and third floors. These explore the many aspects of filmmaking, as well as showcasing movie memorabilia that includes Dorothy's ruby slippers from *The Wizard of Oz*. Iconic items from films are all here, including a surviving Rosebud from *Citizen Kane*. Scripts for blockbusters are dissected and annotated to explain the creative process.

The East West Bank Gallery allows visitors to simulate the experience of walking onto Hollywood's Dolby Theatre stage to accept an Oscar. Other galleries host large-scale temporary exhibitions.

Special Programs

The museum's 1000-seat David Geffen Theater and 288-seat Ted Mann Theater host year-round film screenings and discussions. Oscar Sundays brings out award-winning blockbusters, while Silent Sundays screens long-forgotten classics. Branch Selects sees Academy members curating films significant to their specific craft. Watch for films hosted by academy members who worked on them.

Contrasting Architecture

Designed by Pritzker Prize–winning Italian architect Renzo Piano, the Academy Museum occupies two sharply contrasting buildings. Entry is via the restored Saban Building, a 1939 Streamline Moderne landmark that once housed a May Company department store. Directly behind it is Piano's addition, a commanding space-age sphere featuring a dome with 1500 glass panels. The dome crowns the Dolby Family Terrace, which offers sweeping views of the Hollywood Hills.

★ **Top Tips**

o Download the Academy Museum app, which offers insight to greatly enhance your experience in the galleries.

o Check the museum website for its busy schedule of screenings, including scores of films rarely shown elsewhere. Many titles are geared to families.

✕ **Take a Break**

While the museum is home to a good cafe-restaurant with outdoor seating, you'll find a better range of options at the historic Original Farmers Market (p100), located just 0.5 miles north on Fairfax Ave.

Top Experience 📷

Take in the Wealth of Art at LACMA

The depth and wealth of the collection at the largest art museum in the western US is stunning. LACMA (Los Angeles County Museum of Art) holds all the major players – Rembrandt, Cézanne, Magritte, Mary Cassatt, Ansel Adams – plus millennia worth of Chinese, Japanese, pre-Columbian and ancient Greek, Roman and Egyptian sculpture.

◉ MAP P96, D5

Los Angeles County Museum of Art

lacma.org

P 🚻

Rotating Exhibits

The museum presents an engaging, eclectic mix of exhibitions, with recent offerings including a retrospective on the work and legacy of 16th-century Chinese painter Qiu Ying and the country's largest-ever show dedicated to Fijian art.

Permanent collection highlights include Chris Burden's outdoor installation *Urban Light* (a surreal selfie backdrop of hundreds of vintage LA streetlamps) and Michael Heizer's *Levitated Mass*, a surprisingly inspirational 340-ton boulder perched over a walkway. Other high points: *Cold Shoulder* by Roy Lichtenstein, *Flower Day* by Diego Rivera and *Mulholland Drive* by David Hockney.

Japanese Art Pavilion

LACMA's Zen-like Japanese Art Pavilion (pictured) houses pieces ranging in origin from 3000 BCE to the 21st century. These include Buddhist and Shinto sculpture, ancient ceramics and lacquerware, textiles and armor, and the epic Kasamatsu Shiro woodblock print *Cherry Blossoms at Toshogu Shrine*. The pavilion itself is the work of the late American architect Bruce Goff, known for his organic designs.

Swiss Vision

Demolition of LACMA's mid-century pavilions began in 2020, making way for the David Geffen Galleries, which are the bold vision of Swiss architect Peter Zumthor. His LACMA makeover will see the addition of airy, cantilevered galleries straddling Wilshire Blvd. Floor-to-ceiling windows will make the most of LA's natural beauty, highlighting its hills and celebrated natural light.

★ Top Tip

• Visit on the second Tuesday of the month when admission is free.

• Watch for the opening of the vast David Geffen Galleries in 2024.

✕ Take a Break

LACMA's in-house restaurant **Ray's** (raysandstarkbar.com; P 🛜 🖊 🚹) serves fresh, seasonal fare in an indoor/outdoor venue. Other more casual cafes offer drinks, snacks and sandwiches.

For reviews see

- ⊙ Top Experiences   p92
- ⊚ Sights   p98
- ⊗ Eating   p100
- ⊙ Drinking   p101
- ⊛ Entertainment   p102
- ⊙ Shopping   p103

Melrose Ave

N Sweetzer Ave

Clinton St

N Laurel Ave

N Edinburgh Ave

N Hayworth Ave

N Fairfax Ave

N Genesee Ave

18 ⊡

Rosewood Ave

**BEVERLY
CENTER
DISTRICT**

N La Jolla Ave

N Crescent Heights Blvd

Oakwood Ave

N La Cienega Blvd

7 ⊗

Beverly Blvd

W 1st St

S Edinburgh Ave

S Hayworth Ave

*CBS
Television
City*

4 ⊙

Farmers
Market Pl

W 3rd St

⊙ 12

Gilmour La

⊗ 5

Colgate Ave

S Orlando Ave

S Sweetzer Ave

S La Jolla Ave

S Crescent Heights Blvd

S Fairfax Ave

MID-CITY

N La Cienega Blvd

S San Vicente Blvd

Wilshire Blvd

W 6th St

***Academy
Museum of
Motion
Pictures*** ⊙

LACM

S Corning St

S La Cienega Blvd

Wilshire Blvd

*La Cienega
Park*

S San Vicente Blvd

S Fairfax Ave

⊙ Petersen
Automotive
Museum

1 ⊙

W 8th St

S Ogden Dr

Alandele

W Olympic Blvd

Ⓝ 0 _____ 1 km
0 _____ 0.5 miles

Miracle Mile & Mid-City

E 17 F 11 10 15 G 9 H

Melrose Ave 19

Melrose Ave

MELROSE/
LA BREA

Clinton St

Clinton St

N Stanley Ave
N Curson Ave
N Sierra Bonita Ave
N Gardner St
N Vista St
N Martel Ave
N Fuller Ave
N Poinsettia Pl
N Alta Vista Blvd
N Formosa Ave
N Detroit St
N La Brea Ave

N Sycamore Ave

N Highland Ave

Oakwood Ave

1

2

FAIRFAX
DISTRICT

8

16

Beverly Blvd

Beverly Blvd

HANCOCK
PARK

MID-CITY

W 1st St

S Orange Dr
S Mansfield Ave
S Citrus Ave
N Highland Ave
N McCadden Pl

3

The Grove Dr

Pan
Pacific
Park

S Gardner St
S Vista St
S Martel Ave
S Fuller Ave
S Poinsettia Pl
S Alta Vista Blvd

S Formosa Ave

W 2nd St

W 3rd St

4

W 3rd St

W 3rd St

S Alta Vista Blvd
S Cloverdale Ave
S Detroit St
S La Brea Ave
S Sycamore Ave

W 4th St

S Highland Ave
S McCadden Pl

W 6th St

W 6th St

6

Hancock
Park

La Brea
Tar Pits
& Museum

MIRACLE
MILE

14

Koreatown
(2 miles)

5

2

Wilshire Blvd

Wilshire Blvd

3

Craft
Contemporary

S Stanley
Ave
S Curson Ave

W 8th St

Hauser Blvd
S Ridgeley Dr
S Dunsmuir Ave
S Cochran Ave
S Cloverdale Ave
S Detroit St

S La Brea Ave

W 8th St

13

S Sycamore
Ave

S Citrus Ave
S Highland Ave

6

E W Olympic Blvd F G H

Sights

Petersen Automotive Museum

MUSEUM

1 ◉ MAP P96, D5

A four-story ode to the auto, this is a treat even for those who can't tell a piston from a crankshaft. Inside the museum's body of undulating bands of stainless steel on a hot-rod-red background are four gripping floors exploring the history, industry and artistry of motorized transportation. Regularly changing exhibitions highlight rare, classic and concept cars. The Cars of Film and Television gallery is just that. One floor is devoted to how cars are designed and built. (petersen. org; P ♿)

La Brea Tar Pits & Museum

MUSEUM

2 ◉ MAP P96, E5

Mammoths, saber-toothed cats and other critters roamed LA's savanna in prehistoric times. The tar pits preserve a trove of skulls and bones and are one of the world's most famous fossil sites. Generations of young dino hunters have come to learn about paleontology in the museum. Outside, the smell of asphalt permeates the air as the tar pits still bubble away and beloved models show mammoths stuck in the goo. The surrounding park is a green oasis. LACMA and the Academy Museum are close by.

Thousands of Ice Age critters met their maker between 50,000 and 10,000 years ago in gooey

La Brea Tar Pits Museum

crude oil bubbling up from deep below Wilshire Blvd (though it wasn't Wilshire Blvd then). Animals wading into the sticky muck became trapped and were condemned to a slow death by starvation or suffocation. A life-size drama of a mammoth family outside the museum dramatizes such a cruel fate. Also outside the museum, visitors can observe the pits where fossils are still being discovered. (https://tarpits.org; P 👫)

Craft Contemporary
MUSEUM

3 ◉ MAP P96, E5

This intimate museum showcases both world-renowned and local up-and-coming artists in the folk and craft art worlds. The museum's goal is to straddle the lines between contemporary art, socio-political movements and craft media you don't always see: fiber arts, metalworking, book-binding and more. Hands-on workshops (several family-friendly) help pass along that knowledge.

The gift store is one of the best in town, with hand-crafted gifts, including many by local makers, with an emphasis on jewelry, housewares, textiles and games. (craftcontemporary.org; P 👫)

CBS Television City
STUDIO

4 ◉ MAP P96, D3

North of the Farmers Market is CBS, where game shows, talk shows, soap operas, series and other programs are taped, often

Vibrant Koreatown

Vast and vibrant Koreatown is a platter of sizzling BBQ joints, buzzing malls and karaoke bars, all splashed with a dash of glorious Moderne architecture from the area's gilded past when it was a bastion of Hollywood.

Wilshire Blvd is Koreatown's main east–west thoroughfare. Other strips include 6th St, S Vermont Ave (between Beverly and W Olympic Blvds) and W 8th St (between S Vermont and S Western Aves). The east side abuts lake-studded MacArthur Park, the one that 'melts in the dark' in the eponymous Jimmy Webb song made famous by Donna Summer.

Koreatown has a vast number of eateries. Enjoy soju-fueled grilling marathons at one of Koreatown's countless BBQ joints, among them super-hip and utterly delicious **Ahgassi Gopchang** (kijung.com/ahgassi-gopchang/; P 🛜 👫). Carousing goes far into the night at the many bars and clubs, including classic joints such as **Prince**.

before a live audience, including *Real Time with Bill Maher* and the perennially popular *Price is Right* game show. Check online for tickets. (televisioncityla.com)

Hancock Park

There's nothing quite like the old-money mansions flanking the tree-lined streets of Hancock Park, a genteel neighborhood roughly bounded by Highland, Rossmore and Melrose Aves and Wilshire Blvd.

In the 1920s, LA's leading families, including the Dohenys and Chandlers, hired famous architects to build their pads, and numerous celebrities have lived here amid the curving lawns. It remains popular with the more affluent end of the entertainment industry. It's a lovely area for a stroll or a drive, especially around Christmas when houses sparkle.

Eating

Original Farmers Market
MARKET $$

5 🍴 MAP P96, D3

An atmospheric spot for a casual meal any time of day. The market's covered, open-air walkways are lined with choices, from gumbo and bakery classics to tacos and pizza, sit-down or takeout. There are even a few stalls selling produce! Always good is family-run **Singapore's Banana Leaf** (singaporesbananaleaf.com;), with down-home Southeast Asian cooking.

Fans of Michael Connelly books and *Bosch* will thoroughly enjoy **Du-par's** (dupars.net), a legendary diner with a fine patio. (https://farmersmarketla.com;)

Republique
CALIFORNIAN $$$

6 🍴 MAP P96, G5

Republique sports several fetching hats: artisan bakery, light-filled cafe and buzzing bistro. Scattered with butcher-block communal tables, meat cabinet, marble bar and snug, woody backroom, its open kitchen pumps out daily-changing dishes made with prime produce. Breakfasts and lunches are fresh and casual, while dinners are more serious affairs, with a savvy wine list and unmissable desserts. (republiquela.com;)

Canter's
DELI $$

7 🍴 MAP P96, D2

An old-school deli in the best sense, Canter's has been a fixture in the traditionally Jewish Fairfax district since 1931. Seen-it-all servers deal out pastrami, corned beef and matzo-ball soup, plus plenty of breakfast classics, in a retro space deserving of its own '70s sitcom. (cantersdeli.com;)

Tacos 1986
MEXICAN $

8 🍴 MAP P96, F2

Some of the best – and affordable – meals issue forth from this simple counter-serve stand. The adobo sauce is made with fresh strawberries which give a fresh and sweet tang to the meats it marinates. The carne asada tacos deliver a juicy dose of smoky beef. Get yours *el peron*–style, which features a larger, fresh-flour tortilla that's then fried. (tacos1986.com)

Pink's Hot Dogs HOT DOGS $

9 MAP P96, G1

Famous doggeria (since 1939) with glacially moving lines thanks to the droves who descend for garlicky all-beef frankfurters, painted with mustard, drenched in chili or topped with dozens of combos, some named for celebrities. It also does burgers and fries. (pinks hollywood.com; 👫)

Drinking

Be Bright Coffee COFFEE

10 MAP P96, F1

This popular storefront cafe roasts its own beans, which are used by restaurants across LA. But why go elsewhere? The long list of coffee drinks is expertly crafted and there are also plenty of tea options. (bebrightcoffee.com)

Melrose Umbrella Co COCKTAIL BAR

11 MAP P96, E1

Hit one boutique too many on Melrose? Retreat to the shady back patio of this funky cocktail lounge

Pink's Hot Dogs

and calm your nerves with a piña colada. The namesake umbrellas add color throughout, which goes well with the polychromatic drinks. (melroseumbrellaco.com)

El Carmen
BAR

12 MAP P96, C3

Loud, dimly lit and festooned with bull heads and *lucha libre* (Mexican wrestling) memorabilia, this tequila tavern (over 300 to choose from) pulls an industry-heavy crowd. It's a big hit for weekday happy hour and a top spot to learn the difference between an *añejo* and a *reposado*. Pair the Mexican eats with a tequila cocktail or margarita. (elcarmenla.com)

All Season Brewing Company
BREWERY

13 MAP P96, G6

An old Streamline Moderne Firestone tire store has been reborn as one of LA's best breweries, with a long list of house brews including Bird's Nest Bitter, an English pale ale; Slick, a Baltic porter; Checkered Flag, a saison; and Cloudy Racer, a hazy IPA. Games abound in the airy old garage area and on the patio. (allseasonbrewing.com)

Entertainment

El Rey Theatre
LIVE MUSIC

14 MAP P96, F5

This 1936 art deco dance hall is a brilliant live-music venue, with a killer sound system and excellent

New Beverly Cinema

sightlines. Best of all, it feels truly intimate, even with its 800-person capacity. Acts range from emerging singer-songwriters and rock outfits to big names. (theelrey.com)

Groundlings
COMEDY

15 ⭐ MAP P96, F1

This improv school and company has launched no shortage of top talent, including Lisa Kudrow, Will Ferrell, Maya Rudolph and Melissa McCarthy. Its sketch comedy and improv can be belly-achingly funny, especially on Thursdays when the main company, alumni and surprise guests get to riff together. (groundlings.com)

New Beverly Cinema
CINEMA

16 ⭐ MAP P96, G2

Quentin Tarantino owns the New Bev, a vintage 1920s theater screening classic, cult, current and art films in 35mm, in addition to the Vista Theatre (p63) in Los Feliz. (thenewbev.com; ♿)

Shopping

Melrose Avenue
FASHION & ACCESSORIES

17 🔒 MAP P96, E1

This legendary rock-and-roll shopping strip is as famous for its epic people-watching as it is for its retail pleasures. The strip between N Poinsettia Pl and N Fairfax Ave gets a lot of the buzz thanks to the boutiques stuck together like block-long hedgerows. Most of its

gear is rather low-end, so if you're after the hipper, higher-end stuff, explore the long stretch between N Crescent Heights Blvd and N Almont Dr, or hit 3rd St.

Reformation
FASHION & ACCESSORIES

18 🔒 MAP P96, C1

Reformation is celebrated for its frocks, tops, jumpsuits, denim and more, pieces that meld simplicity, style and killer sass. Most pieces are part of limited-edition collections and all are designed and made in LA. The brand prides itself on using sustainable and vintage fabrics and environmentally responsible production practices. (thereformation.com)

Slow
VINTAGE

19 🔒 MAP P96, E1

Vintage shoppers flock here for specs and hats, sun dresses from the '60s, some groovy tweeds and ragged old army threads. It specializes in one-of-a-kind pieces and leather goods. (☎323-944-0195)

The Grove
MALL

20 🔒 MAP P96, D3

LA's most famous alfresco mall pulls in everyone from locals and tourists to the odd celebrity. Complete with fountain-studded piazza, vintage-style trolley and a movie-set feel, its retailers include Nordstrom and a full slate of mid-range and upscale chains. (thegrovela.com; 🛜♿)

Walking Tour 🚶

Culver City Shuffle

Hollywood's workaday sibling, Culver City has played a major role in the city's entertainment industry, its studios churning out scores of movie and TV classics. Now a burgeoning tech hub, it's one of LA's underrated pleasures: a livable, vibrant neighborhood where Hollywood history meets polished hipness and comfort.

Walk Facts

Start Platform; Ⓜ E Line to Culver City

End Sony Pictures; Ⓜ E Line to Culver City

Length 1 mile; two hours

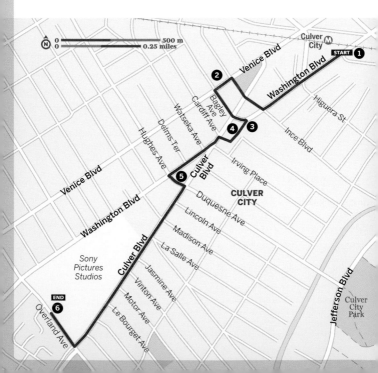

❶ Platform

Culver City's cool factor is exemplified by Platform, a buzzing outdoor development that harbors niche fashion and lifestyle boutiques, trendy cafes and eateries. Stop by **Loqui** (eatloqui.com) for fast and creative Mexican you can enjoy on the back patio.

❷ Something Strange

Hidden behind an inconspicuous door, the **Museum of Jurassic Technology** (MJT; mjt.org; 🚻) is LA's most idiosyncratic museum. It has nothing to do with dinosaurs or technology. Instead, its labyrinth of curiosities would be right at home in a carnival sideshow, which may be the idea.

❸ Culver Studios

Many iconic movies were filmed at **Culver Studios**, including the original *A Star is Born*. Now home to Amazon Studios, its landmark Colonial-Revival mansion – once the office of producer David O Selznick – is featured in the opening credits of *Gone With the Wind*, also filmed on site.

❹ Culver Hotel

A National Historic Landmark, the 1924 **Culver Hotel** is where 124 actors portraying Munchkins slept three-to-a-bed while filming *The Wizard of Oz*. The 1939 movie classic was shot at the nearby MGM Studios (before Sony bought it). From here, Washington Blvd is lined with many shady cafes.

❺ Kirk Douglas Theatre

A striking example of Streamline Moderne architecture, the **Kirk Douglas Theatre** (centertheatre group.org) began life in 1946 as a movie palace. It has since been recast as a playhouse showcasing new works by local playwrights.

Across the intersection, **Village Well Books** (villagewell.com) is a gem of a small shop, with hordes of writers pounding on keyboards at the communal tables.

❻ Sony Pictures & the Ghosts of MGM

Arguably the most storied of the old major studios, MGM was not in Hollywood, but right here in Culver City. Today it's known as Sony Pictures (Amazon owns the rights to the name!) and you can visit the location where films such as *The Wizard of Oz*, *Ben-Hur*, *Men in Black* and *Spider-Man* were shot. Countless TV series also use the studio, including *Jeopardy*. In-depth **tours** (sonypicturesstudios tours.com) depart from Overland Gate on Overland Ave.

Explore

Santa Monica

Santa Monica is LA's little sister, its smaller, beachier twin, with glass towers abutting the famous pier and amusement park. Surrounded by the city on three sides and the Pacific on the fourth, in 'SaMo' boarders bob in the waves, real-life Lebowskis sip white Russians next to martini-swilling Hollywood producers, and celebrity chefs rub elbows with soccer moms at bountiful farmers markets.

The Short List

○ **Palisades Park (p112)** *Savoring sweeping bay views and glorious sunsets.*

○ **Santa Monica Pier (p108)** *Strolling to the end, then riding the roller coaster, Ferris wheel and antique carousel.*

○ **Santa Monica Farmers Markets (p114)** *Snaffling up the region's best produce – after all, this is where the chefs shop.*

○ **Marvin Braude Bicycle Trail (p109)** *Pedaling along the ocean for miles and miles.*

○ **Bergamot Station Arts Center (p112)** *Wandering through 30 galleries, exhibiting the works of superb photographers and artists.*

Getting There & Around

Ⓜ The E Line (Gold) train takes about 50 minutes from DTLA.

🚌 Metro Bus 4 follows Santa Monica Blvd through Beverly Hills and Hollywood to DTLA. Santa Monica's municipal Big Blue Bus travels around town and to the LAX Transit Center.

Neighborhood Map on p110

Top Experience 📷

Enjoy Amusement Park Fun on Santa Monica Pier

No visit to LA is complete without a stroll on this historic pier that features on just about every LA tourist ad. There are arcades, carnival games, a vintage carousel, a Ferris wheel, a roller coaster and an aquarium, plus snack stands, fancier restaurants and vendors selling crafts and schlock.

◎ MAP P110, A5

santamonicapier.org

Pacific Park

Everyone gets their kicks on Santa Monica Pier at this classic **amusement park** (pacpark.com; 👥), with rides out of a county fair, like a famous Ferris wheel, a tame roller coaster, midway games and food stands.

Santa Monica Pier Carousel

The charming 1922 National Historic Landmark **Santa Monica Pier Carousel** (📞310-394-8042; 👥) at the beginning of the pier has 44 horses (plus one rabbit and one goat), a calliope and a traditional soda fountain.

The Beach

There are endless ways to enjoy this oh-so-wide 3.5-mile **stretch of sand** (www.smgov.net/portals/beach), running from Venice Beach in the south to Will Rogers State Beach in the north. Sunbathing and swimming are obvious options, but you can also reserve time on a beach volleyball court and work out at the **Original Muscle Beach** (santamonica.com/things-to-do/original-muscle-beach-santa-monica/) with its ropes, parallel bars and swings.

South Bay's Bicycle Trail

The fabulous **Marvin Braude Bicycle Trail** (beaches.lacounty.gov/la-county-beach-bike-path/; 👥) parallels the sand for most of the 22 miles between Will Rogers State Beach on the north end of Santa Monica and Torrance County Beach in the south. There are numerous bike rental shops along the beaches.

★ Top Tips

∘ The rides at the old-fashioned, family-friendly Pacific Park costs a fraction of a visit to Disneyland and Universal Studios Hollywood.

∘ The pier extends almost a quarter-mile over the Pacific. It was the end of the iconic Route 66, which began at Grant Park in Chicago.

∘ Beachside parking fees add up quickly. Take the Metro instead.

✗ Take a Break

Dogtown Coffee (dogtowncoffee.com) is in the old Zephyr surf-shop headquarters, where skateboarding was invented during the 1970s. It brews great coffee and makes a mean breakfast burrito, the preferred nutritional supplement of surfers the world over. Fun fact: Dogtown was the boarders' nickname for southern Santa Monica and Venice.

Santa Monica

500 m
0.25 miles

1

Annenberg
Community
Beach House 3

Palisades Park

Palisades Ave
Alta Ave

Montana Ave

Idaho Ave
Washington Ave

14th St

Euclid St
26

15th St
16th St
17th St
18th St
19th St
Montana Ave

20th St
21st St

California Ave

Wilshire Blvd

20th St

Arizona Ave

16

23

Santa Monica Blvd

17th St
18th St
19th St

Broadway

Colorado Ave

14th St

Euclid St
12th St
11th St
10th St
9th St

15th St
16th St

12th St
11th St
14 10th St

31
11
25

Bay Cities
Italian Deli
& Bakery

Lincoln Blvd

Lincoln
Park

Lincoln Blvd

7th St

7th St
10

6th St
5th St
4th St
3rd St
2nd St
1st Ct

Montana Ave
Idaho Ave
Washington Ave
California Ave
Palisades Ave

Palisades
Park

21

6th St
5th St
Wilshire Blvd
4th St

Arizona Ave

Third Street
Promenade

9
27
12

2nd St

5th St
4th St

22
28 24

Santa Monica Place

Santa Monica Broadway

Santa Monica Blvd
17

Ocean Ave

Ocean Ave

Pacific Coast Hwy

Santa Monica
Information
Kiosk

Santa Monica State Beach

Palisades Park

Santa Monica

For reviews see	
◉ Top Experiences	p108
◎ Sights	p112
✕ Eating	p114
✕ Drinking	p117
✿ Entertainment	p118
🛍 Shopping	p119

◎ ✕ ✕ ✿ 🛍

Bergamot Station
Arts Center (800m)

5 ↗ ↗ 15 ⊗

Pico Blvd

Santa Monica College

Pearl St

Santa Monica Fwy

Woodlawn Cemetery

16th St

14th St

14th St

Memorial Park

Cove Skatepark ◉ 8

Olympic Blvd

Euclid St

Euclid St

Bay St

Pearl St

Pine St

Ocean Park Blvd

11th St

Colorado Ave

10th St

Lincoln Blvd

Lincoln Blvd

Santa Monica High School

6th St

Hollister Ave

Hill St

Ashland Ave

Pico Blvd

4th St

4th St

3rd St

Main St

◉ 5 Edgemar
✕ 18

◎ 4 California Heritage Museum

◎ 29

30

Neilson Way

Main St

✕ 13

20

Main St

Bike Center ◉ 7
Santa Monica

ⓘ

6 ◎ Poseidon

◉ 19

Ocean Ave

Bay St

Barnard Way

South Bay Bicycle Trail

Heal the Bay
Aquarium 1 ◉

◉ Santa Monica Pier

Santa Monica Bay

Santa Monica State Beach

A

B

C

D

E

F

5

6

7

8

Sights

Heal the Bay Aquarium
AQUARIUM

1 ◉ MAP P110, A5

Under the Santa Monica Pier – just below the carousel – is this small aquarium, sponsored by the environmental group Heal the Bay. Kid-friendly touch tanks crawl with crabs and crustaceans scooped from local waters. Get close to an eel in the reef area and see seaweed up close in an exhibit on the kelp forests growing just offshore. (healthebay.org/aquarium; 🚼)

Palisades Park
PARK

2 ◉ MAP P110, B3

This gorgeous cliffside park is perched dramatically on the edge of the continent's front yard. Stretching 1.5 miles north from the pier, the palm-dotted greenway

---

Bergamot Station Arts Center

A former trolley yard and warehouse complex, **Bergamot Station Arts Center** (bergamotstation.com; **P**) is one of LA's best arts centers. More than 30 private galleries show the works of well-regarded (and even famous) artists and photographers. The free exhibitions are always changing, so the best way to see things is just to wander around.

---

sees a mix of joggers and tourists who have come to take in the ocean and pier views. Sunsets are priceless. (☎800-544-5319)

Annenberg Community Beach House
BEACH

3 ◉ MAP P110, A1

Like a fancy beach club for the rest of us, this sleek and attractive city-owned spot, built on the estate of actress Marion Davies (the longtime mistress of William Randolph Hearst), opens to the public on a first-come, first-served basis. It has a lap pool, lounge chairs, yoga classes, beach volleyball, fitness room and art gallery. You can also tour the neo-classical Davies house.

This part of the beach was known as the Gold Coast in the 1920s and '30s, when celebrities like Davies and others had their beachside estates here. Think of it as an early Malibu. Cary Grant lived at 1039 Palisades Beach Rd with his close friend Randolph Scott. (annenbergbeachhouse.com)

California Heritage Museum
MUSEUM

4 ◉ MAP P110, B7

For a trip back in time, check out the exhibits at this museum, which is housed in one of Santa Monica's few surviving grand Victorian mansions – this one was built in 1894. Curators do a wonderful job presenting pottery, colorful tiles, Craftsman furniture, folk art, vintage surfboards and other fine

BERZAD MOLOUD/SHUTTERSTOCK ©

California Heritage Museum

collectibles in dynamic fashion. It has regular art shows. (california heritagemuseum.org; P)

Edgemar
NOTABLE BUILDING

5 ◉ MAP P110, B7

This former dairy plant was redesigned and adpated by Frank Gehry, whose signature LA work is Walt Disney Concert Hall (p144). It's a relatively early design from the 1980s, but you'll see signature poured-in-place concrete, metal fencing and a soaring tower. (edgemar.com)

Poseidon
WATER SPORTS

6 ◉ MAP P110, B5

Ever wondered what it feels like to be one of those bad-asses pad-dling the long board beyond the break and then riding the swell? Then find this little nook of a shop south of the pier. It sells and rents surfboards and stand-up paddle-boards and can set you up with lessons, too. (poseidonstandup.com)

Bike Center Santa Monica
CYCLING

7 ◉ MAP P110, B5

This city-operated outfitter has lots of different types of bikes, from cruisers to tandem to elec-tric, as well as wheelchairs and strollers. It also hands out useful bike maps of the Westside and offers excellent themed walking and cycling tours. (thebike center.com)

The Baywatch Beach

It's one of the most common questions from fans of bad TV: is the vast expanse of Santa Monica's beach where they filmed *Baywatch*? Despite the show's premise – that David Hasselhoff, Pamela Anderson and the rest spent their time saving swimmers from sharks and serial killers in Santa Monica – most exterior scenes were filmed 3 miles northwest at Will Rogers State Beach, which is generally quieter and more salubrious for TV production.

Cove Skatepark   SKATEBOARDING

8 ◉ MAP P110, E5

This is the place modern skateboarding was invented, and skate rats will love the 20,000 sq ft of vert, street and tranny terrain in the city-operated Memorial Park. There's street, bowl, mini-ramp and pool skating. (facebook.com/TheCoveSkateparkofSantaMonica)

Eating

Santa Monica Farmers Markets   MARKET $

9 ✕ MAP P110, B4

You haven't really experienced Santa Monica until you've explored one of its outdoor farmers markets stocked with organic fruits, vegetables, flowers, baked goods and prepared foods. The big dog is the legendary Wednesday market – it's the biggest and the best for fresh produce, and is the hunting ground for leading chefs from across Southern California.

The Saturday morning market is more of a community scene, with live music and plenty of stalls selling breakfast foods. Just hand your bicycle to the valet (it's free!) and relax with the locals (and the odd slumming celeb) on the lawn. (www.smgov.net/portals/farmers market; ♿)

Cassia   SOUTHEAST ASIAN $$$

10 ✕ MAP P110, C4

Open, airy Cassia has made about every local and national 'best' list of LA restaurants. Chef Bryant Ng draws on his Chinese-Singaporean heritage in dishes such as *kaya* toast (with coconut jam, butter and a slow-cooked egg), 'sunbathing' prawns and the encompassing Vietnamese pot-au-feu: short-rib stew, veggies, bone marrow and delectable accompaniments. The wine list is superb.

Even the building is cool – the 1937 art deco Santa Monica Telephone Building. (cassiala.com; Ⓟ)

Mélisse   FRENCH $$$

11 ✕ MAP P110, D3

When a special event demands something extraordinary, the two-star Mélisse is the perfect solution. Chef Josiah Citrin leads a superb kitchen team at this tasting room, which operates within his namesake one-star restaurant Citrin. Only a handful of diners get to embark on the adventure, where bold flavors are melded with modern French techniques. The wine pairings and service are exceptional. (citrinandmelisse.com)

Élephante

ITALIAN $$$

12 🍴 MAP P110, B4

Grand ocean views from a breezy rooftop are the immediate draw. But the delectable small plates, pasta dishes and nicely charred individual pizzas will eventually draw your attention away from the palm-tree-fringed vistas. It's a stylish scene – sunset is sublime – and the odd celeb confirms that A-listers like a good view as much as anyone. (elephantela.com)

Sunny Blue

JAPANESE $

13 🍴 MAP P110, B8

In Japan, *omusubi* (rice balls, aka *onigiri*) are an everyday staple, and this counter-service shop aims to make them popular Stateside. Before your eyes, the cheerful staff stuffs fluffy rice with dozens of fillings like miso beef and spicy salmon, then wraps it in a crunchy *nori* seaweed wrapper. Veggie-friendly options include miso mushroom and hijiki seaweed. (sunnyblueinc.com;)

Santa Monica Seafood

SEAFOOD $$

14 🍴 MAP P110, D3

One of the top seafood markets in Southern California offers a tasty oyster bar and sit-down market

Santa Monica Seafood

Godmother of All Sandwiches

The signature sandwich at **Bay Cities Italian Deli & Bakery** (Map p110, D4; baycitiesitalian deli.com; P) – the best Italian deli in LA, period – is the sloppy, spicy Godmother (piled with salami, mortadella, capicola, ham, prosciutto, provolone and pepper salad). It also has house-roasted tri-tip, eggplant parmigiana, tangy salads, fresh breads, imported meats, cheeses and oils to salivate over. The outdoor seating is meh, so we take ours to the beach. Save time by ordering ahead.

cafe, where you can sample delicious chowder, salmon burgers, albacore melts, oysters on the half shell and pan-roasted cod. It's been in business since 1939 but feels totally up-to-date and has good sustainable cred. (smseafood market.com; P)

Birdie G's   AMERICAN $$

15 MAP P110, F5

Influences at chef Jeremy Fox's casual eatery range from Europe to the American South to the Golden State itself. It's comfort food with color and flair, and everything is served with a heartwarming down-home sensibility. There's a fun kids menu and even the dessert list is delightfully whimsical. It's close to the Bergamot Station Arts Center (p112). (birdie gsla.com)

Milo & Olive   ITALIAN $$

16 MAP P110, F3

Small-batch wines, incredible wood-fired pizzas, terrific breakfasts (creamy polenta and poached eggs) and homemade breads and pastries are all part of the allure at this cozy neighborhood joint. Enjoy meals at the marble bar, shoulder to shoulder with new friends at a common table or out on the lovely patio. (miloandolive.com)

Mercado   MEXICAN $$

17 MAP P110, C4

Come at happy hour for the exquisite carnitas tacos made with slow-cooked pork and slathered with guacamole. Otherwise, this is upscale dining, so expect sleek common tables and leather booths, plus a selection of grilled steaks and seafood similar to what you might get at a Mexican resort. It mixes excellent margaritas and has a killer tequila list. (cocinasy calaveras.com)

Holey Grail Donuts   BAKERY $

18 MAP P110, B7

In a region known for great donuts, the Holey Grail manages to stand out. The dough is made with taro flour sourced from Hawai'i and then fried in coconut oil. The result? A sweet treat loaded with island goodness. There are over 60 flavors to choose from, and all the ingredients are ethically sourced. (holeygraildonuts.com)

Drinking

Chez Jay   BAR

19 MAP P110, B5

Since 1959, this nautical-themed dive (yes, there is a wooden ship's wheel) has seen its share of Hollywood intrigue from the Rat Pack to the Brat Pack. It remains dark and dank and all the more glorious for it. The classic steak and seafood menu's not bad, either (many love the calamari). The year-round holiday lights may have you singing Christmas carols no matter the month. (chezjays.com)

Library Alehouse   PUB

20 MAP P110, B8

You can almost hear the ocean – you can definitely smell it – at this Ocean Park gastropub where locals gather for the food as much as the beer. Choose from a long list of local microbrews on tap while you hang on the cozy outdoor patio. Burgers, fish tacos and hearty salads offer familiar and high-quality eats. (libraryalehouse.com)

Penthouse   ROOFTOP BAR

21 MAP P110, B3

On the 18th floor of the Huntley Hotel is the highest bar in Santa Monica Bay, with sweeping views. There's a high-end menu of food for hotel guests, but the real reason to come here is to gaze out across Southern California and the Pacific while sipping a creative cocktail. (thehuntleyhotel.com/penthouse/nightlife)

Bar Chloe   LOUNGE

22 MAP P110, B4

Bar Chloe is cozy, dark and elegant with dangling chandeliers, twinkling candles, intimate booths, crisp white tablecloths and a chamomile mai tai that has earned rave reviews. It makes its own syrups and juices using farmers market (p114) produce, and there's a simple menu of burgers, cheese plates and fries. (barchloe.com)

10 Speed Coffee   COFFEE

23 MAP P110, F4

This industrial-chic coffee bar is the place to fuel up on caffeine before a big ride, and there are always lots of bikes locked up in front. Seating abounds, whether you're in a group or flying solo. Beans are single-origin and roasted in micro-batches. (www.10speed coffee.com)

Entertainment

Harvelle's
BLUES

24 ⭐ MAP P110, C4

This dark blues grotto has been packing 'em in since 1931, but somehow still manages to feel like a well-kept secret. There are no big-name acts here, but the quality is usually high. Sunday's Toledo Show mixes soul, jazz and cabaret, and other nights might bring jam sessions or burlesque shows. (santamonica.harvelles.com)

Broad Stage
THEATER

25 ⭐ MAP P110, D4

At the 499-seat, state-of-the-art Broad (rhymes with 'road'), the lineup of touring shows covers everything from new interpretations of classic Shakespeare to one-man productions, edgy plays and classical and world-music performances. It's the headline venue of Santa Monica College's performing arts programs. (broad stage.org)

Aero Theater
CINEMA

26 ⭐ MAP P110, E1

Since 1940 the alluring neon marquee of the Aero has lured in moviegoers. Now operated by the nonprofit American Cinematheque, it screens classics and offers programs with industry luminaries. It's the home for the LA edition of the beloved Noir City series. (americancinematheque.com)

Aero Theater

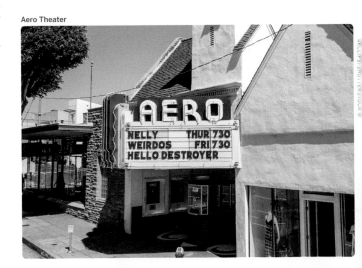

Laemmle Monica Film Center
CINEMA

27 ⭐ MAP P110, B4

Current, tasteful and thought pro-voking art-house films are screened in this spiffy multiplex a block off the Promenade. (laemmle.com)

Shopping

Puzzle Zoo
GAMES

28 🔒 MAP P110, C4

Those searching galaxy-wide for the caped Lando Calrissian action figure, look no more. Puzzle Zoo stocks every imaginable *Star Wars* or anime figurine this side of En-dor. There's also an encyclopedic selection of puzzles, board games and toys. Kids (and many adults) adore it. (puzzlezoo.com; 🚻)

Jadis
GIFTS & SOUVENIRS

29 🔒 MAP P110, B8

Don't miss this homespun, steampunk-paradise museum and shop, grinding with old gears and spare-part robots, antique clocks, concept planes and cars, old globes and lanterns – many of which were film props (it calls itself a 'mad scientist prop house'). Toys, games and other ephemera feature the same quirky aesthetic. (jadisprops.com)

Ten Women
ART

30 🔒 MAP P110, B8

This longstanding gallery sells art, folk art and crafts from a coopera-tive of 28 (it used to be 10) female artists. Always changing, but look for works in ceramic, wood, tex-tiles, jewelry and more. (tenwomengallery.com)

Great Labels
FASHION & ACCESSORIES

31 🔒 MAP P110, D3

Sensational secondhand couture and designer hand-me-downs from celebrity consigners. There are Oscar and Golden Globe gowns, elegant handbags, shoes and accessories from Pucci, Prada, Jimmy Choo and Dior. If you've ever wanted to pay $250 for a four-figure dress, come here. (greatlabels.com)

SaMo Shopping

Covering three long blocks of downtown Santa Monica, between Broadway and Wilshire Blvd, **Third Street Promenade** (Map p110, B4) offers carefree, car-free strol-ling amid topiaries, fountains and street performers. **Santa Monica Place** (Map p110, B4; santamonicaplace.com), just south of the Promenade, offers upscale chains.

For locally owned boutiques, try high-end **Montana Ave**, north of downtown, and fun-and-funky **Main St**, heading south into Venice.

Santa Monica Shopping

Explore ⊕

Venice

Come down to the Boardwalk and inhale an incense-scented whiff of Venice: a boho beach town and long-time haven for artists, New Agers, road-weary tramps, skateboarders and free spirits. This is where Jim Morrison and the Doors lit their fire, Arnold Schwarzenegger pumped himself to stardom and Dennis Hopper finally settled down. Even as tech titans move into restored homes along the famous canals, the Old Venice spirit endures.

The Short List

○ **Venice Boardwalk (p122)** *Witnessing street performers, fortune tellers, muscle men and bewildered tourists all having fun by the beach.*

○ **Abbot Kinney Blvd (p127)** *Strolling and shopping America's coolest street.*

○ **Venice Canals (p127)** *Admiring intimate homes around the waterways that lend Venice its name.*

○ **High Rooftop Lounge (p130)** *Sipping a seasonal cocktail and marveling at the views from this rooftop lounge by the ocean.*

○ **Venice Skatepark (p123)** *Watching skateboarders catch air – you may even feel airborne yourself.*

Getting There & Around

Ⓜ The E Line to Downtown Santa Monica is a nice beach stroll 1.5 miles north.

🚌 Metro Bus Line 33 and Santa Monica's Big Blue Bus Lines 1, 3 and 18. Line 3 connects to the LAX City Bus Center.

Neighborhood Map on p126

Top Experience 📷

Get in on the Action on Venice Boardwalk

Prepare for a sensory overload on Venice's Board-walk, a one-of-a-kind experience. Buff bodybuild-ers brush elbows with street performers and sellers of sunglasses, ribald underwear, Mexican ponchos and cannabis, while cyclists and in-line skaters whiz by on the bike path, and skateboard-ers and graffiti sprayers get their own domains.

 MAP P126, A3

Ocean Front Walk

Murals

Venice Beach has long been associated with street art, and for decades there was a struggle between outlaw artists and law enforcement. Art won out and the tagged-up towers and the free-standing concrete wall of the **Venice Beach Art Walls** (veniceartwalls.com; 🚻), right on the beach, have been covered by graffiti painters from 1961 to the present.

Muscle Beach

Gym rats with an exhibitionist streak can get a tan and a workout at this famous **outdoor gym** (laparks.org/venice/muscle-beach-venice-outdoor-gym) right on the Venice Boardwalk, where Arnold Schwarzenegger and Franco Columbu once bulked up. Nearby volleyball nets and basketball courts also get a workout.

Venice Skatepark

When Angelenos drained their swimming pools during a 1970s drought, board-toting teens from Venice and neighboring Santa Monica made their not-quite-welcome invasion and modern skateboarding culture was born. Today, this public, 17,000-sq-ft, ocean-view **skate park** (veniceskatepark.com) is a destination for both high flyers and gawking spectators. There are regular competitions. Look for great photo ops, especially as the sun sets.

★ **Top Tips**

● The Boardwalk is busiest on summer weekend afternoons, especially for the Sunday afternoon drum circle.

● Off-season, around sunset, crowds gather at cafes, bars and on the bike path.

● Late nights and early mornings are quietest. Head south from Venice Pier for the emptiest sands.

✕ **Take a Break**

No place melds Old Venice and New Venice like the **Rose** (therosevenice.la; 🅿 🚻). This airy institution dates from 1979 yet remains current, serving a diverse, all-day menu (sophisticated pastries to gourmet feasts) to laptop-toting writers, tech geeks and Gold's Gym beefcakes.

Walking Tour 🥾

The Venice Stroll

Step into the Venice lifestyle and rub shoulders with folks who believe that certain truths will only be revealed to those who disco-skate in a Speedo-and-turban ensemble.

Walk Facts

Start Venice Pier; 🚌 Culver City Bus Line 1, Metro Line 33

Finish Abbot Kinney Blvd; 🚌 Big Blue Bus Line 18

Length 3.5 miles; two hours

❶ South Venice Beach

While other piers along the coast have more action, the beach around the **Venice Pier** is about as calm as it gets around these parts. The typical Venice crowds dissipate, golden sands unfurl and beach volleyball games break out at a moment's notice.

❷ Venice Canals

This idyllic neighborhood preserves 3 miles of **waterways** (p127) lined with eclectic homes, conceived by Venice's founder Abbot Kinney. Today it's a warren of cool waterside houses with cute little gardens and boats tied up out front. Exit the enclave and turn left at S Venice Blvd.

❸ Venice Boardwalk

The famed **Venice Boardwalk** (p122) is a vortex for the loony, the free-spirited, the hip and the athletic. Turn right down Ocean Front Walk.

❹ Muscle Beach

Six-pack stomachs and rippling abs abound at this outdoor **gym** (p123) on the boardwalk. Now it's part workout space, part voyeuristic delight.

❺ Venice Beach Art Walls

Make sure you have your camera at the tagged-up towers and concrete verticals of **Venice Beach**

Art Walls (p123), forever open to aerosol artists.

❻ Venice Skatepark

This **skatepark** (p123) is an irresistible lure to skate punks and spectators, thanks to vert, tranny and street terrain with unbroken ocean views.

❼ Waterfront

At the indoor-outdoor beach bar **Waterfront** (thewaterfrontvenice. com), hipsters, surfers and shamblers rub elbows, quaffing beers, wines and coffees.

❽ Ballerina Clown & Binoculars Building

Where Rose Ave meets the beach, head inland to two Venice landmarks. Jonathan Borofsky's *Ballerina Clown* dances above Main St. Diagonally across is the **Binoculars Building** (p127).

❾ Abbot Kinney Boulevard

From Main St, turn left onto **Abbot Kinney Blvd** (p127), the street brimming with boutiques and restaurants.

✕ Take a Break

Put your feet up at one of the many cafes and restaurants along Abbot Kinney Blvd. For a quick bite, try the takeout counter at **Gjelina** (p129).

Venice

A1

B1

C1

D1

A2

B2

C2

D2

A3

B3

C3

D3

A4

B4

C4

D4

A5

B5

C5

D5

A6

B6

C6

D6

0   400 m
0   0.2 miles

Rose Ave

Hampton Dr

3rd St

4th St

7th Ave

Rose

Rose Ave

Café
Gratitude

5th Ave

6th Ave

5 Binoculars
Building

3 Gold's Gym

Sunset Ave

Pacific Ave

Main St

2nd St

11

Vernon Ave

Indiana Ave

Ocean Front Walk

Speedway

Brooks Ave

Venice
Beach

21

Broadway St

Homage to
Starry Night

8 Electric Ave

Abbot Kinney Blvd

Westminster Ave

San Juan Ave

12

Venice
Boardwalk

Westminster Ave

10 Abbot
Kinney
Boulevard

Santa Clara Ave

22

Venice
Reconstituted

San Juan Ave

24

20

California Ave

Linus
(1km)

9 17

15

Market St

Windward Ave

1 25

13

7

Palms Blvd

Jim Morrison
Mural

VENICE

Venice Way

Grand Blvd

Mildred Ave

Dell Ave

14

Electric Ave

Abbot Kinney Blvd

4

4 LA Louver

N Venice Blvd

S Venice Blvd

18

Santa
Monica
Bay

Speedway

Pacific Ave

2 Canal Park
Venice
Canals

Venice Canals

Venice Way

South Bay Bicycle Trail

South Venice
Beach

19

Venice Pier

23

Dell Ave

Washington Blvd

6
Marina Del Rey
Parasailing

For reviews see

⦿ Top Experiences p122
◉ Sights   p127
✕ Eating   p129
🖢 Drinking   p130
🔒 Shopping   p132

Sights

Abbot Kinney Boulevard

AREA

1 ⊙ MAP P126, C4

Abbot Kinney, who founded Venice in the early 1900s, would probably be delighted to find that one of Venice's best-loved streets bears his name. Sort of a seaside Melrose with a beachy flavor, the mile-long stretch of Abbot Kinney Blvd between Venice Blvd and Main St is full of upscale boutiques, galleries, lofts and top cafes and restaurants. Many shops are housed in reconstructed old wooden beach shacks.

Venice Canals

AREA

2 ⊙ MAP P126, B5

Even many Angelenos have no idea that just a couple of blocks from the Boardwalk madness is an idyllic neighborhood that preserves 3 miles of Abbot Kinney's canals. The **Venice Canal Walk** threads past eclectic homes, over arching bridges and along waterways where ducks preen, artists paint and locals lollygag in little rowboats or sip cocktails on little barges moored in front of their cute homes. It's best accessed from either Venice or Washington Blvds.

Gold's Gym

GYM

3 ⊙ MAP P126, C2

There are gyms, then there's Gold's Gym, and *then* there's the original 1965 Gold's, the self-titled

Beachfront Murals

Venice's collection of building murals is superb and includes these works by Rip Cronk: a shirtless **Jim Morrison** (Morning Shot; Map p126, A4; 1881 Speedway) plus homages to Van Gogh's **Starry Night** (Map p126, B3; Ocean Front Walk, at 5 Wavecrest Ave) and Botticelli's **Birth of Venus** (Map p126, B4; 25 Windward Ave), titled *Venice Reconstituted*.

'Mecca of Bodybuilding.' Generations have been lifting at the place that arguably started the fitness craze – Arnold Schwarzenegger trained here for the iconic 1977 muscle-mania film *Pumping Iron*. (goldsgym.com/veniceca)

LA Louver

GALLERY

4 ⊙ MAP P126, B4

One of LA's best galleries, LA Louver was established by Peter Goulds in 1975, and since 1994 has been housed in a landmark building designed by Frederick Fisher. It's a modern and contemporary art gallery featuring rotating, museum-quality exhibitions. Summer hours are limited. (lalouver.com)

Binoculars Building

NOTABLE BUILDING

5 ⊙ MAP P126, B1

Originally the headquarters for the Chiat\Day advertising agency

Fun in the Sun

You're never far from places to rent gear at Venice Beach. You'll find businesses out on the sand in huts and also along Ocean Front Walk. Typical items on offer include bikes in all flavors, surfboards, boogie boards, lounging chairs and umbrellas.

(Apple et al), this Frank Gehry–designed office building is now home to Google and, thanks to its eye-catching architecture and the Claes Oldenburg and Coosje van Bruggen sculpture out front (clue to its design in the name), makes for a fun photo stop on the north end of Venice.

Marina Del Rey Parasailing

WATER SPORTS

6 MAP P126, C6

Immediately south of Venice, Marina Del Rey Parasailing will harness you in and have you flying up to 500ft high – or for more cash, even higher. It's a quick thrill: flights last eight to 12 minutes, but the views can be stunning. You start in the marina harbor that was used for the iconic opening credits of *Gilligan's Island* and its departure on a three-hour tour. (marinadelreyparasailing.com)

The Butcher's Daughter

Eating

Gjelina
AMERICAN $$

7 MAP P126, D4

If one restaurant defines Venice today, it's this. Carve out a spot on the communal table, or get your own slab of wood on the expansive and elegant stone terrace, and dine on imaginative small plates and sensational thin-crust, wood-fired pizza. By day, the breakfasts feature fresh crusty bread and reimagined old standards. (gjelina.com)

Felix Trattoria
ITALIAN $$$

8 MAP P126, C3

Watch skilled chefs creating new types of pasta – in both shapes and composition – right before your eyes. Choice California ingredients are combined for artful and seasonal Italian fare. Don't miss the *sfincione*, a Sicilian take on focaccia. (felixla.com)

Teddy's Red Tacos
MEXICAN $

9 MAP P126, B4

Birria is all the rage in LA. The long-simmered, piquant Mexican stew usually made from beef (but traditionally from goat) is being sold from taco trucks and top-end restaurants alike. Teddy's was one of the first to catch the wave, and its *birria* is considered foundational by LA's Mexican food cognoscenti. The tacos and platters here are best enjoyed at the outdoor tables. (teddysredtacosofficial.com)

La Vida Vegan

Venice is LA's vegan capital, and most restaurants like Butcher's Daughter will have plenty of vegan options. However places like **Café Gratitude** (Map p126, C1; cafegratitude.com;) set new standards with artfully presented vegan cooking.

The Butcher's Daughter
VEGETARIAN $$

10 MAP P126, C3

Find yourself a seat around the central counter or facing busy Abbot Kinney to tuck into stone-oven pizzas, handmade pastas and veggie faves such as whole roasted cauliflower and butternut-squash risotto. Light, airy and fun. The coffee is excellent and vegans are well accommodated. (thebutchersdaughter.com)

Gjusta
CALIFORNIAN $$

11 MAP P126, C2

A very casual, very gourmet, *very* local bakery, cafe and deli behind a nondescript storefront on a hidden side street. The menu changes regularly, but expect to be surprised by the combinations of flavors and inventive presentation. The patio is one of the Venice spaces you won't want to leave. (gjusta.com)

Bike Like a Venetian

Bikes rule the roadways in Venice and one shop rules the competition. **Linus** (linusbike. com), the ultimate Venice bike hub, assembles sturdy, steel-frame bikes. Can't carry a bike home with you? It also sells covet-worthy accessories such as bike bags, baskets, cup holders and even beer holsters.

The Wee Chippy   FISH & CHIPS $

12 ⊗ MAP P126, A3

Definitely a chip or two ahead of the other fast-food options on the boardwalk, the Wee Chippy churns out excellent fish and chips to the happy masses. The fish is cod (unless you opt for vegan or shrimp) and the potatoes are not quite fully peeled and then fried perfectly crisp – no limp, soggy chips here! (weechippy.com)

Salt & Straw   ICE CREAM $

13 ⊗ MAP P126, D4

There always seems to be a line out the door at this ice-cream fantasy land. Maybe it's because there's always something new to try (adventurous, seasonally themed flavors change monthly, anything from the farmers market is fair game) in addition to year-round classics. (saltandstraw.com)

Superba Food & Bread   CALIFORNIAN $$

14 ⊗ MAP P126, D4

This industrial-sleek, indoor-outdoor space on a popular stretch of Lincoln Blvd has fab breads and pastries (all to go), excellent coffees and flawless California cooking. For breakfast, avocado toast delights those unafraid of clichés. Lunch brings salads and sandwiches, and dinner adds bigger plates. Vegetarians are well served. (lifesuperba.com/venice -menu/; P ❄)

Drinking

High Rooftop Lounge   ROOFTOP BAR

15 ⊕ MAP P126, B4

From its sprawling 5th-floor location,,Venice's most popular rooftop bar boasts 360-degree views which stretch from the shore to the Santa Monica Mountains. High serves inventive seasonal cocktails and small dishes (charcuterie boards, tacos, flatbread-style pizzas) to keep you sated between rounds. Reservations recommended. (highvenice.com)

Venice Ale House   PUB

16 ⊕ MAP P126, A1

A fun pub right on the Boardwalk at Venice's north end, blessed with ample patio seating for sunset people-watching, long boards suspended from the rafters, rock on the sound system, plenty of local brews on tap and organic bar chow. (venicealehouse.com)

Townhouse & Del Monte Speakeasy BAR

17 🍷 MAP P126, B4

Upstairs is a cool, dark and per- fectly dingy bar with pool tables, booths and a history that dates back to 1915. Downstairs is the speakeasy, where DJs spin pop, funk and electronic music, comics take the mic and jazz players set up and jam. A good time almost any night. (townhousevenice.com)

Brig BAR

18 🍷 MAP P126, D5

Once a divey pool hall, Brig now has a spiffed-up mid-century

vibe and attracts a trendy mix of grown-up beach bums, arty professionals and professional artists. Watch the Abbot Kinney people parade from the outside tables where food trucks gather. (thebrig.com)

Hinano Cafe BAR

19 🍷 MAP P126, B6

Wearing its dive bar label proudly, Hinano has been serving up beer and wine to boozers with sand on their feet since 1962. Jim Mor- rison was a regular, back when he was somewhere between bum and songwriter. The burgers are fine, the pool tables busy and the views pure gold. (hinanocafe venice.com)

The Wee Chippy

Shopping

Aviator Nation
CLOTHING

20 🔒 MAP P126, C4

This beachwear brand's flagship and original store sells coastal-chic hoodies, tees and blankets. Behind the store is an awesome chill space with a DJ station and games, all done up in the brand's trademark yellow, orange and red stripes. (aviatornation.com)

Burro
GIFTS & SOUVENIRS

An Abbot Kinney fave, Burro (see 13 ✕ Map p126, D4) deals in quality aromatherapy candles, art books, a smattering of boho-chic attire for ladies, fair-trade beach bags from India and beaded jewelry. (burrogoods.com)

Kiss Kiss Tattoo
BODY ART

21 🔒 MAP P126, B3

Don't be the last person in Venice to have a tattoo. This top-end storefront has artisans who will art up your body and add a piercing or three. It's the antithesis of the grungy tattoo parlor, with a welcoming vibe and plenty of suggestions and advice. (kisskiss tattoo.com)

Small World Books
BOOKS

22 🔒 MAP P126, A3

Get your best beach read here. Tucked behind a cafe, this used and new bookstore has fab staff recommendations and an appealing and eclectic selection. (smallworldbooks.com)

Venice Canals (p127)

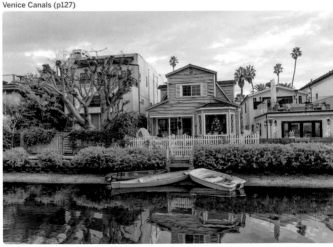

A Brief History of Venice

In 1905, Abbot Kinney, a tobacco mogul by trade and a dreamer at heart, dug canals and turned fetid swampland into a cultural and recreational resort he dubbed the 'Venice of America.' For nearly two decades, crowds thronged to this Coney Island on the Pacific to be poled around by imported gondoliers, walk among Renaissance-style arcaded buildings and listen to Benny Goodman tooting his horn in clubs. Most of the canals were filled and paved over in 1929, after which Venice plunged into a steep decline until its cheap rents and mellow vibe drew first the beatniks and then the hippies in the '50s and '60s. These days, tech and entertainment dollars have fueled a hard-charging gentrification that has made Venice one of the most desirable areas in LA.

Arbor Venice   SPORTS & OUTDOORS

23 🔒 MAP P126, B6

This local maker started out with snowboards and has since branched out to skateboards, the outfits that go with them (using materials such as bamboo and organic cotton) and gear. A portion of the profits go to rainforest restoration in Hawai'i. (arborcollective.com)

Strange Invisible Perfumes   PERFUME

24 🔒 MAP P126, C3

Organic, intoxicating perfumes crafted from wild and natural ingredients, with names such as Aquarian Rose and Fair Verona; many are gender neutral. Atlantic is an artful composition of frank-incense, sandalwood, rum and peppermint. (siperfumes.com)

Principessa   FASHION & ACCESSORIES

25 🔒 MAP P126, C4

An affordable and worthy boutique with sporty denim and skirts, jewelry and droopy hats, baby-doll dresses, scarves, sequined boots and purses. And in case you need some essentials for your holiday, they've got sleek bikinis and negligees, too. (principessavenice.com)

Walking Tour 🚶

Manhattan Beach, Sand and More

A bastion of surf music and the birthplace of beach volleyball, Manhattan Beach may have gone chic, but that salty-dog heart still beats. Yes, the downtown area along Manhattan Beach Blvd has seen an explosion of trendy restaurants and boutiques, but the real action is beachside, where the bikinis are small, the waves kind and the smiles as oversized as those sunglasses.

Getting There

🚗 Access Manhattan Beach via the Imperial Hwy to Vista Del Mar; it's the most scenic route.

🚌 Beach Cities Transit 109

❶ Sweat & Tumble

Sand Dune Park (citymb.info; 🚹) requires reservations to access the long, deep 100ft-high natural sand dune, but the nature trail with California native shore plants is worth the effort. Follow 33rd St down to one of LA's best beachfront walks.

❷ Righting an Injustice

Founded in 1912, **Bruce's Beach** was a popular African American private beach. Driven by racism, the town of Manhattan Beach seized the beach from the Bruce family in 1924. In 2022, LA County returned the area bounded by Highland Ave and 27th St to the family, who then sold it back to the county so it can continue to serve as the popular public park it is today. Markers recall the saga.

Return to the beachfront walkway, admiring the surf and the striking beachfront homes.

❸ Hit the Beach

Ditch the shoes on the wide sweep of golden sand at **Manhattan Beach** (citymb.info). You'll find pick-up volleyball courts, a pier with sweeping blue sea views, and a consistent sandy bottom surf.

❹ Photo Bomb

No surf, sport or music nut should miss the dazzling work on display at **Bo Bridges Gallery** (bobridges gallery.com), off 11th St. Bridges made his name photographing the likes of Kelly Slater.

❺ Ice Cream Addiction

Hordes queue out the door of **Manhattan Beach Creamery** (mbcreamery.com) for its sublime frozen joy.

❻ MB Post

Trendy but unvarnished, **MB Post** (eatmbpost.com; 🚹) offers farm-to-table fare. Dine at the long communal tables in the bar or reserve a more intimate table in the dining room.

❼ Ercoles 1101

A funky counterpoint to MB's stylish bars, **Ercoles** (https://ercoles1101.com) is a dark, chipped, well-irrigated dive with a barn door open to everyone from salty barflies to Gen Z pub crawlers and volleyball stars.

Explore

Downtown

Take Manhattan, add a splash of Mexico City, a dash of Tokyo, shake and pour. Your drink: Downtown LA. Rapidly evolving, DTLA is the city's most intriguing patch, where cutting-edge architecture and elite modern-art museums contrast sharply with blaring mariachi tunes, Chinese grocers, abject poverty, old architectural gems and scores of hot restaurants, bars, galleries and boutiques.

The Short List

○ **Broad (p138)** *Musing on modern masterpieces at a cutting-edge art museum.*

○ **Walt Disney Concert Hall (p144)** *Catching a symphony in a Frank Gehry–designed showstopper.*

○ **Grand Central Market (p148)** *Sampling multicultural bites in a vibrant food market.*

○ **Rooftop bars (p150)** *Sipping Manhattan-style at rooftop bars like Perch.*

○ **Los Angeles Music Center (p152)** *Catching a performance at the USA's top performing arts complex.*

Getting There & Around

Ⓜ Downtown has two subways: the B/D lines and the new A/E lines. They all converge at the 7th St/Metro Center station. The A/B/D lines interchange with Metrolink commuter trains and Amtrak at historic Union Station.

🚌 Metro buses connect Downtown to much of LA. DASH buses run five routes through Downtown.

Neighborhood Map on p142

Grand Central Market (p148) LET GO MEDIA/SHUTTERSTOCK ©

Top Experience

Marvel at the A-List Art at Broad

What do you do when you've got too much art to handle? Build a cutting-edge museum, fill it with your blockbuster acquisitions and share it with the city. That's exactly what LA philanthropist and billionaire real-estate mogul Eli Broad and his wife Edythe did, and their 2000-strong collection is considered one of the world's most prominent holdings of postwar and contemporary artworks.

◎ MAP P142, E2

thebroad.org

P 🚻

Collections

The first thing you should do at the Broad (rhymes with 'road') is register your name for a viewing of *Infinity Mirrors*, an extraordinary LED installation by Japanese artist Yayoi Kusama. Wait times can exceed an hour, though you're free to browse the museum until your viewing time, announced via text message. From the lobby floor, a 105ft escalator ascends through a space-gray cavity to the 3rd floor, where visitors are greeted by Jeff Koons' giant stainless-steel tulips.

The surrounding galleries rotate works from the Broad's permanent collection, whose strengths lie in classic 1960s pop art. Important works from this era include Robert Rauschenberg's JFK-themed *Untitled*, part of a series that saw Rauschenberg become the first American to win the Grand Prize at the Venice Biennale.

Architecture

The museum building is as much a talking piece as the collection within. Costing $140 million, the 120,000-sq-ft showpiece was designed by New York's Diller Scofidio + Renfro, in collaboration with SF-based firm Gensler. It's 'shrouded' in a white lattice-like shell, complete with a 'dimple' (an oculus looking out onto Grand Ave) and corners that lift sharply at street level to let art lovers and the curious in and out.

Inside, the building bucks the museum tradition of hiding away its storage facilities. Here, 'The Vault' becomes an integral part of the design experience. Hovering between the 1st- and 3rd-floor galleries, it's pierced by the escalator connecting the gallery floors and visible through glass panels, offering visitors a voyeuristic peek at museum artworks lying dormant.

★ Top Tips

◦ Reserve a timed entrance online; the line for same-day walk-ups can be long.

◦ Viewings of Yayoi Kusama's *Infinity Mirrors* installation can book out; try to visit in the morning. Check your phone regularly, as wait times are sometimes shorter than estimated.

◦ Download the excellent Broad smartphone app, an audio guide that offers insightful information on the art and artists. It includes a tour for kids narrated by LaVar Burton.

★ Take a Break

Chef Timothy Hollingsworth (ex-French Laundry) helms **Otium** (http://otiumla.com; 🛜), a fun, sophisticated hot spot, set in a modernist pavilion beside the Broad.

Walking Tour 🥾

Ghosts of Downtown

Downtown is the most historical and fascinating part of Los Angeles. Its streets are awash with the dreams of architects, designers and stars, translated into an extraordinary cache of buildings both breathtaking and whimsical. Thread your way through its multilayered streets to discover the treasures of Downtown's gilded past and its unsettled future.

Walk Facts

Start Eastern Columbia Building; M A/B/D/E Lines to 7th St/Metro Center

Finish Los Angeles Central Library; M B/D Lines to Pershing Sq

Length 1 mile; two hours

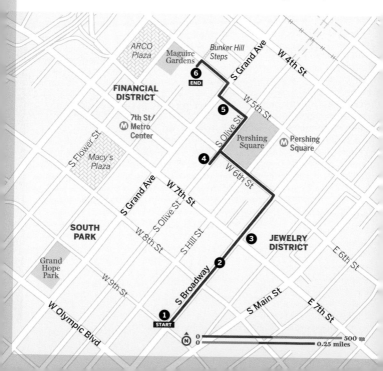

❶ Eastern Columbia Building

Rising at the corner of 9th St and Broadway, the 13-story **Eastern Columbia Building** (eastern columbiahoa.com) is a masterpiece of art moderne architecture, clad in highly glazed turquoise-and-gold terracotta tiles and featuring a gilded sunburst vestibule. Completed in 1930, its clock-tower top is a landmark.

❷ Broadway Theatre District

Spanning eight blocks of S Broadway from 11th St to 3rd St, the Broadway Theatre District once claimed the highest concentration of movie palaces in the world. The grand venues are in varying states of repair, but look for the marquees of the Belasco, Mayan, Orpheum and the restored Million Dollar Theatre, among others.

At number 630, the **Palace Theatre** (https://thedowntownpalace.com) dates from 1911 and featured in Michael Jackson's *Thriller* video. Across Broadway, the lavish Los Angeles Theatre hosted the premiere of Charlie Chaplin's silent film *City Lights*.

❸ Clifton's Republic

Opened in 1935, this was the **flagship cafeteria** (theneverlands.com/cliftons-republic/) of restaurant owner and social reformer Clifford Clifton. The son of missionaries, he founded organizations such as Meals for Millions and ran his cafe-terias under his golden rule: diners should only pay what they thought was fair and no one should ever be turned away hungry. In his spare time, he funded efforts to clean up LA's squalid and corrupt politics.

❹ James Oviatt Building

From 1928 to 1967, Olive St's **James Oviatt Building** was home to fabled men's clothing store Alexander & Oviatt. Upon completion, the building's art deco lobby forecourt sparkled with 30-plus tons of glass by René Lalique, who also designed the mailboxes, directories and dashing doors of the time-warped elevators.

❺ Millennium Biltmore Hotel

The Academy Awards were founded in 1927 at the **Millennium Biltmore Hotel** (thebiltmore.com; P @ 🛜 ✂). The hotel's Historic Corridor features a fascinating photograph of the 1937 Oscars. Its screen credits are lengthy, including *Chinatown*, *Beverly Hills Cop* and even *Bachelor Party*.

❻ Los Angeles Central Library

Designed by Bertram Grosvenor Goodhue, Downtown's **central library** (lapl.org/branches/central-library; 👥) opened in 1926. Head straight for the second floor to admire at its basilica-like rotunda, surrounded by the California-themed murals of Dean Cornwell in Technicolor.

A

22

Chick Hearn Ct

Grammy Museum

3

B

Francisco St

C

Wilshire Blvd

D

Pasadena Fwy

1

S Figueroa St

S Flower St

S Hope St

W 12th St

W 11th St

ARCO Plaza

Grand Hope Park

SOUTH PARK

S Grand Ave

Macy's Plaza

7th St/ Metro Center

Maguire Gardens

W 5th St

W 4th St

2

S Olive St

S Hill St

W Olympic Blvd

W 9th St

24

W 8th St

20

Bar Clara

S Grand Ave

FINANCIAL DISTRICT

Pershing Square

S Broadway

S Main St

23

Upstairs at the Ace Hotel

JEWELRY DISTRICT

S Broadway

Pershing Square

Perch

21

S Los Angeles St

California Market Center

S Spring St

16

W 6th St

W 5th St

26

W 4th St

3

Santee St

27

Maple Ave

Wall St

FASHION DISTRICT

12

S Main St

18

Cole's

15

10

E Olympic Blvd

E 11th St

E 10th St

E 9th St

E 8th St

Flower Market

E 7th St

E 6th St

4

San Julian St

S San Pedro St

San Julian St

Winston St

E 5th St

Crocker St

Towne Ave

Stanford Ave

ARTS DISTRICT

5

E 12th St

E Olympic Blvd

E 7th St

S 6th St

6

S Central Ave

25

Warehouse St

19

E 7th St

S Central Ave

S Alameda St

E 6th St

E 5th St

Palmetto St

A

B

C

D

For reviews see

◉	Top Experiences	p138
◎	Sights	p144
✖	Eating	p147
🍷	Drinking	p150
✪	Entertainment	p151
🔒	Shopping	p152

Sights

MOCA
Grand Avenue

MUSEUM

1 ◉ MAP P142, E2

MOCA's notable art collection focuses mainly on works created from the 1940s to the present. There's no shortage of luminaries, among them Mark Rothko, Dan Flavin, Willem de Kooning, Joseph Cornell and David Hockney, in regular and special exhibits. Check to see if there are temporary exhibitions at the **MOCA Geffen** in Little Tokyo. (Museum of Contemporary Art; moca.org; 👫)

Walt Disney
Concert Hall

CULTURAL CENTER

2 ◉ MAP P142, E2

A molten blend of steel, music and psychedelic architecture, this iconic concert venue is the home base of the **Los Angeles Philharmonic**, but also hosts contemporary acts and jazz performances. The 2003 concert hall's star architect, Frank Gehry, played every note to the hilt to produce a gravity-defying sculpture of heaving and billowing stainless steel. (laphil.org; P)

Grammy Museum

MUSEUM

3 ◉ MAP P142, B1

The highlight of the **LA Live** (lalive. com) entertainment complex, this museum's interactive exhibits

Union Station

TOMS AUZINS/SHUTTERSTOCK ©

LA's Architectural Masterpiece

Built on the site of LA's original Chinatown, **Union Station** (Map p142, G4; unionstationla.com; P) opened in 1939 as America's last grand rail station. It remains one of LA's architectural masterpieces, its Mission Revival style infused with both art deco and Native American accents. Today, it's a vibrant facility, serving as a hub for Metro, Metrolink and Amtrak trains.

The station even houses its own microbrewery, **Homebound Brew Haus** (Map p142, G4; homeboundbrewhaus.com; 📶), which occupies a glorious, sprawling hall with original Navajo-inspired floor tiles. And there's a beer garden.

explore the evolution of popular music and the famous awards. Rotating exhibits might include iconic threads worn by Whitney Houston, Peggy Lee and Beyoncé, scribbled words from the hands of Count Basie and Taylor Swift, and instruments once played by music legends. It also has performances by top talent. (grammymuseum. org; P 👫)

El Pueblo de Los Ángeles Historical Monument

HISTORIC SITE

4 ⊙ MAP P142, G3

A short stroll northwest of Union Station, this compact, colorful district is where LA's first colonists settled in 1781. Wander through narrow **Olvera St's** vibrant and family-owned Mexican-themed stalls and check out the district's museums, the best of which is **LA Plaza** (La Plaza de Cultura y Artes; lapca.org; 👫), offering snapshots of the Mexican American experience

in Los Angeles. The **Avila Adobe** (elpueblo.lacity.org), built in 1818, is one of LA's oldest buildings. The eye-opening **Museum of Social Justice** (museumofsocialjustice. org) looks at local history through the filters of poverty, women's suffrage and civil rights. (elpueblo. lacity.org; 👫)

Japanese American National Museum

MUSEUM

5 ⊙ MAP P142, F4

Anchoring the vibrant Little Tokyo neighborhood and dedicated to the Japanese immigrant experience, this impressive museum includes the 'Common Ground' exhibition, which explores the evolution of Japanese American culture since the late 19th century. Exhibits give moving insight into the mass incarceration of over 125,000 American citizens of Japanese descent in remote internment camps during WWII. (janm.org; 👫)

LA's Stunning New River Crossing

Opened in 2022, the striking **6th Street Viaduct** runs for over two-thirds of a mile, connecting Downtown's Arts District with the Boyle Heights neighborhood in East LA. Its overall design has been lauded and won fans from the start. Looping concrete arches in huge and varying sizes cross the Los Angeles River and two freeways at varying angles, while helical ramps accommodate cyclists.

It's an ever-changing and vibrant look for what could have been a humdrum design. The previous viaduct was a beloved location used in myriad films and TV shows, including *Repo Man*, *Terminator 2: Judgment Day* and *Drive*.

Los Angeles City Hall
HISTORIC BUILDING

6 ◎ MAP P142, F3

Until 1966 no LA building stood taller than the 1928 City Hall, which appeared in the *Dragnet* TV series and 1953 sci-fi thriller *War of the Worlds*. On clear weekdays you'll have views of the city, the mountains and several decades of Downtown growth from the 27th-floor **observation deck**. On the way up, stop off on level three to eye City Hall's original main entrance, which features a breathtaking Byzantine-inspired rotunda graced with marble flooring and a mosaic dome. (📞213-485-2121; 🚻)

Bradbury Building
HISTORIC BUILDING

7 ◎ MAP P142, E3

Debuting in 1893, the Bradbury is one of LA's heritage jewels. Behind its Romanesque-lite facade lies a whimsical galleried atrium that wouldn't look out of place in New Orleans. Inky filigree grillwork, rickety birdcage elevators and yellow-brick walls glisten golden in the afternoon light, which filters through the peaked glass roof. Such striking beauty hasn't been lost on Hollywood; it's been used in hundreds of productions, including *Blade Runner*. (laconservancy.org/locations/bradbury-building)

Biddy Mason Memorial Park
MONUMENT

8 ◎ MAP P142, E3

Stretching along a green and inviting alley behind the Bradbury Building and across from Grand Central Market, this historical display details the incredible life of Biddy Mason. Born an enslaved person in Mississippi in 1818, Mason eventually moved to Cali-

...fornia where she won a landmark court case in 1856 confirming her freedom. Working as a nurse, she began buying land – including this part of DTLA – and became a philanthropist to African Americans, the poor and the sick.

Angels Flight

CABLE CAR

9 👁 MAP P142, E2

Built in 1901, this funicular originally shuttled commuters between Downtown and the long-gone Victorian abodes that graced Bunker Hill. The top end is fairly soulless and corporate, but the ride is an excursion into LA's past. Fans of Michael Connelly's books and the *Bosch* TV series will get extra thrills. (angelsflight.org; 🚹)

Eating

Bar Amá

TEX-MEX $$

10 ✖ MAP P142, D3

Bar Amá cooks up smashing, sophisticated Tex-Mex meals. Lick lips and fingers over queso (a creamy melted cheese) with chorizo; slow-roasted beef belly with cotija cheese, tomatillo and pomegranate; and a not-to-be-missed roasted cauliflower with cilantro pesto. The place knows how to craft a cocktail. (bar-ama.com)

Bavel

MIDDLE EASTERN $$$

11 ✖ MAP P142, E6

Sleek, loud and showered in cascading vines, Bavel's clean, modern takes on Middle Eastern

Angels Flight

Ramen Hood

classics are phenomenal. The chefs draw on their backgrounds in Israel, Turkey, Egypt and Morocco to create delicious and surprising combinations, followed by pastry-driven desserts. Superb cocktails seal the deal. (baveldtla. com; P 📶 🖊)

Sonoratown TACOS $

12 🍴 MAP P142, B3

One of LA's best cheap eats straddles the Fashion District and DTLA. This packed taqueria pumps out superb northern Mexican street food. The buttery tortillas – made in-house using lard and specialty Sonoran flour – are a worthy match for the succulent, mesquite-grilled meats. (sonora town.com; 🚻)

Sushi Gen SUSHI $$

13 🍴 MAP P142, E5

Come super early to grab a lunch seat at this exceptional sushi spot, where Japanese chefs carve thick slabs of *toro* (tuna belly), Japanese snapper and more. While the sushi counter serves à-la-carte options, your goal is an actual table, where you can enjoy the great-value sashimi. Dinner is a less frenetic, more mannered affair. (sushigen dtla.com; P)

Grand Central Market

Designed by Union Station architect John Parkinson, LA's beaux arts **Grand Central Market** (Map p142, E3; grandcentralmarket.com; 🎧) is a neon-splashed bustle of counters peddling everything from artisan cheeses to oysters and BBQ. If you're undecided, opt for carnitas tacos from **Villa Moreliana** (📞213-725-0848; 🚻), pretty much any breakfast item from **Eggslut** (eggslut.com; 🎧🚻) or the vegan tonkatsu at **Ramen Hood**. The much-loved LA coffee chain **G&B Coffee** (gget.com) started here and it remains the location where it tries out new ways to work caffeinated magic.

Cole's or Philippe's?

Among the myriad foods LA can claim to have invented (the hot fudge sundae, the cheeseburger, the California roll), one of the oldest is the French Dip sandwich, the 1908 concoction of soft French bread piled with sliced lamb, beef, turkey, pork or pastrami and dipped in beef au jus. Today, two surviving vets of the era both claim parentage: **Cole's** (Map p142, C3; colesfrenchdip.com; 📞) and **Philippe the Original** (Map p142, H3).

Who first sliced and dipped what first is hotly debated; even more controversial is which barebones joint serves the *better* French Dip. We'll leave it to you to decide, but we give Cole's points for its hot and garlicky 'atomic pickles,' while Philippe's gets credit for its spicy mustard.

Pearl River Deli
CHINESE $$

14 🍽 MAP P142, H3

Chef Johnny Lee works his magic at this buzzing Cantonese restaurant in Chinatown. In fact, he figuratively pulls his dishes out of a hat – you never know what will be on the menu and that incredible fave you had this week (crab omelet, porkchop bun) may leave the lineup and never return. Open for lunch only around the weekend (check!). (instagram.com/prd_la/)

Orsa & Winston
FUSION $$$

15 🍽 MAP P142, D3

Progressive, well-executed Italian-Asian fusion flavors the five-course tasting menus here. Chef Josef Centeno turns dinner into an adventure with seasonal ingredients prepared in new and surprising ways. Seafood from the nearby Pacific often features, as does pasta made in-house. Even the ever-elusive abalone can make an appearance. Optional wine pairings. (orsaandwinston.com)

Gelateria Uli
ICE CREAM $

16 🍽 MAP P142, D3

Uli Nasibova's small-batch gelato is the bomb. Made with seasonal, locally sourced ingredients, flavors find their muse in LA's cacophony of neighborhoods reflecting the world's cultures. Lick a San Gabriel Valley–inspired black sesame, a Filipinotown-channeling *ube* (purple yam) or Thai Town coconut-and-lemongrass. The silky consistency and sheer clarity of flavor is inimitable. (ulisgelato.com; 🍴 👪)

Downtown Rooftop Toasts

Downtown makes the most of its taller-than-average buildings with a slew of buzzing rooftop bars. Top picks include fancy-pants **Perch** (Map p142, D2; perchla.com; 📶), a multi-level bar-restaurant crowning the 13th floor of the Renaissance Revival Pershing Square Building.

Alternatively, head to **Upstairs at the Ace Hotel** (Map p142, B2; acehotel.com/los-angeles/; 📶), a stylish 14th-floor hangout with a luxe, safari-inspired fit-out. The pool is open to all; on weekend afternoons a DJ spins tunes.

The former Giannini Building opened in 1922 and became home to the Bank of America. Today it's the Hotel Per La and up top on the 12th floor is **Bar Clara** (Map p142, C2; hotelperla.com/bar -clara/), a rooftop pool bar with extravagant murals, cocktails and views.

Drinking

Endorffeine COFFEE

17 🚇 MAP P142, H3

Jack Benchakul brings his Thai background to a busy Chinatown mall where he creates all manner of coffee drinks with Southeast Asian twists. And he's no absentee visionary; he brews every drink himself. Beans come from a rotating lineup of LA's best small roasters. (endorffeine.coffee)

Varnish BAR

18 🚇 MAP P142, C3

Tucked into the back of Cole's (p149) is this dark, friendly speakeasy, an essential and award-winning downtown bar. Perch at the bar or slip into a booth and trust the staff's impeccable suggestions. Live music (anything from funk to tiki) strikes up Sunday to Wednesday. As part of the throwback vibe, it's cash only. (thevarnishbar.com)

Everson Royce Bar COCKTAIL BAR

19 🚇 MAP P142, C6

Don't be fooled by the unceremonious gray exterior. Behind that wall lies a hopping Arts District hangout, with a buzzy, bulb-strung outdoor patio. The barkeeps are some of the city's best, using craft liquor to concoct drinks such as the prickly pear Mateo Street margarita. Bar bites are equally delightful – the shrimp toast is a treat. (erbla.com)

Ham & Eggs Tavern
BAR

20 MAP P142, C2

This rock 'n' roll dive has it all: affable barkeeps, decent beer and vino, and a gritty, house-party vibe channeling Downtown pre-gentrification. It's tiny, dark and loud, serving up live rock and punk to an eclectic crowd of partiers. Masked behind the shopfront of a defunct Chinese diner, it's easy to miss.

Precinct
GAY

21 MAP P142, D3

Climb the stairs to this sprawling, dimly lit, down-n-dirty, rock-and-roll-style bar where Downtown gays frolic in a series of bars, dance floors and an indoor-outdoor play-pen. Friday and Saturday are club nights. (precinctdtla.com)

Entertainment

Crypto.com Arena
STADIUM

22 MAP P142, A1

South Park got its first jolt in 1999 with the opening of this saucer-shaped sports and entertainment arena, formerly known as the Staples Center. It's homecourt for the Los Angeles **Lakers** (nba.com/lakers), **Clippers** (nba.com/clippers) and **Sparks** (https://sparks.wnba.com) basketball teams, and home ice for the **LA Kings** (nhl.com/kings). The stadium also hosts pop and rock concerts and the odd political convention. Outside on Star Plaza are statues of famous LA athletes, including Magic Johnson, Wayne Gretzky, Shaquille O'Neal and Elgin Baylor. (cryptoarena.com)

Crypto.com Arena

MARCUS E JONES/SHUTTERSTOCK ©

Downtown Entertainment

United Artists Theatre

LIVE PERFORMANCE

23 ⭐ MAP P142, B2

A historic gem of a 1600-seat movie palace restored by the Ace Hotel, which curates the calendar. Offerings are eclectic, ranging from hip-hop, indie and spoken-word performances to internationally prolific comedy acts. The interior is a Spanish Gothic fantasy dating to 1927. It was designed with the help of the original UA partners, the silent-era legends Mary Pickford and Douglas Fairbanks. (The Theatre at Ace Hotel; https://acehotel.com/los-angeles/theatre)

Rooftop Cinema Club DTLA

CINEMA

24 ⭐ MAP P142, B2

It's cinema under the stars – at least they're supposed to be up there in the smoggy, nighttime glare. A mix of current blockbusters and classics (*Casablanca*) are screened year-round at this 4th-floor terrace atop the Level Hotel. Find a comfy Adirondack chair (built for one or two) and sit back with a microbrew, regional wine or cocktail. Food choices are basic. (rooftopcinemaclub.com/los-angeles/venue/dtla)

Shopping

Row DTLA

SHOPPING CENTER

25 🔒 MAP P142, B6

Row DTLA has transformed a sprawling industrial site into a curated garden of specialty retail and dining delights. Saunter pe-destrianized streets for discerning apparel and accessories, designer homewares, niche fragrances and even Japanese bicycles. Top picks include Japanese-accented sta-tionery purveyor **Hightide Store**

Los Angeles Music Center

The county-owned **Los Angeles Music Center** (Performing Arts Center of Los Angeles County; Map p142, F2; musiccenter.org) complex is one of America's largest performing arts centers. Its multiple venues – **Walt Disney Concert Hall** (p144), the **Dorothy Chandler Pavilion** (musiccenter.org), the **Mark Taper Forum** (centertheatregroup.org) and **Ahmanson Theatre** (centertheatregroup.org) – host resident companies including Center Theatre Group, Los Angeles Master Chorale, Los Angeles Opera and the Los Angeles Philharmonic.

Plazas with sculptures and a grand fountain link the venues. Before the advent of the Disney and its accompanying hoopla, the Chandler was LA's major performing arts venue and was the site of the Oscars for nearly 30 years.

Santee Alley

DTLA (hightidestoredtla.shop), the impossibly beautiful and picturesque floral boutique **Jean-Pascal Florist Studio** and Micah Cohen's progressive unisex fashion label **Shades of Grey** (shadesofgrey clothing.com; 📶 🚻)

Last Bookstore · BOOKS

26 🔒 MAP P142, D3

California's largest new-and-used bookstore spills across two sprawling levels of an old bank building. You'll find everything from cabinets of rare books to an upstairs horror-and-crime book vault, book tunnel and smattering of art galleries. The store also houses

a terrific vinyl collection and cool store-themed merch. Prices are reasonable, staff recs superb. (lastbookstorela.com; 🚻)

Santee Alley · FASHION & ACCESSORIES

27 🔒 MAP P142, A3

Santee Alley is packed with solid bargains spanning everything from denim, dresses, shoes and baseball caps to cell-phone covers, bling, eyewear and fragrances. Over 150 shops and stalls are found in alleys between Santee Street and Maple Avenue, from Olympic Blvd to 12th Street. (https://fashiondistrict.org/santee -alley; 🚻)

Top Experience

Explore Three Great Museums at Exposition Park

A quick jaunt south of Downtown, family-friendly Expo Park began as an agricultural fairground in 1872 and has been a patch of public greenery since 1913. Today's draws are a trio of great museums and the Los Angeles Memorial Coliseum, which has hosted two Olympics and is home to the USC Trojans college football team.

https://expositionpark.
ca.gov

California Science Center

There's plenty to see at this multistory **museum** (californiasciencecenter.org; 🚹) filled with interactive exhibits. A simulated earthquake is among the crowd-pleasers, and the star attraction, the Space Shuttle *Endeavour*, will be back on display in the huge Samuel Oschin Air and Space Center sometime after 2025.

Natural History Museum

From dinos to diamonds, this **museum** (nhm.org; P 🚹) takes you around the world and through eons. A huge new wing, NHM Commons, will open in 2024. Among the features is Gnatalie, a long-necked dinosaur measuring over 70 feet long.

California African American Museum

CAAM (caamuseum.org; P 🚹) showcases African American artists and the African American experience, with a special focus on California and LA. Exhibits change throughout the year in galleries around a sunlit atrium.

Los Angeles Memorial Coliseum

Built in 1923, this grand 77,500-seat **stadium** (pictured; lacoliseum.com) hosted the Summer Olympic Games twice (1932, 1984) and will do so again in 2028. Informative guided tours dish the history, show off recent renovations and take you inside locker rooms, the field and more.

★ **Top Tips**

• Get lost in the Natural History Museum's 3.5-acre nature gardens, with over 600 species of plants.

• When the NHM's popular butterfly pavilion is open, buy advance tickets to ensure entry.

• **Lucas Museum of Narrative Art**, founded by *Star Wars* creator George Lucas, is set to open in 2025.

✕ **Take a Break**

A five-minute walk under the freeway, the fabulous food hall **Mercado La Paloma** (mercadolapaloma.com; P) has a dozen stalls selling everything from Yucatan cuisine to Thai.

★ **Getting There**

🚌 Ten minutes from Downtown LA on the Metro E Line (Gold) to Expo Park/USC.

🚗 Take the Vermont Ave exit off the I-10 Fwy.

Walking Tour 🥾

Old & New in Pasadena

Pasadena is imbued with old-school Americana, meaning it has a certain genteel comfort that you'll easily sense along its immaculate streets, where gnarled native oaks shade gracious arts-and-crafts mansions. Color comes from some top museums and lively Old Pasadena, a bustling 20-block downtown shopping and entertainment district of historic brick buildings.

Getting There

Ⓜ Metro A Line (Blue) light rail serves Pasadena and connects it to Downtown LA and Long Beach. Metro bus line 256 serves the Rose Bowl.

🚗 Take CA-110 from Downtown.

❶ Circle the Rose Bowl

The venerable 1922 **Rose Bowl Stadium** (rosebowlstadium.com) seats up to 92,500 spectators and shines every New Year's when it hosts the Rose Bowl college football game. The surrounding Brookside Park is nice for hiking, cycling and picnicking. Families can check out the excellent **Kidspace Children's Museum** (kidspacemuseum. org; P ♿).

❷ Tour the Gamble House

There's exquisite attention to detail at the **Gamble House** (https://gamblehouse.org; P), a 1908 masterpiece of Craftsman architecture built by Charles and Henry Greene for Procter & Gamble heir David Gamble. Incorporating 17 types of wood, art glass and subdued light, the entire home is a work of art.

❸ Enjoy World-Class Art

Rodin's *The Thinker* is only an overture to the full symphony of art at the exquisite **Norton Simon Museum** (nortonsimon.org; P). User-friendly galleries teem with choice works by Rembrandt, Renoir, Van Gogh and many other A-List painters. The Asian sculpture collection is superb.

❹ Idiosyncratic Interest

Amid the mainstream shopping scene in Old Pasadena is this treasure chest of a boutique filled with surprising and unlikely arts and crafts items. **Gold Bug** (goldbugpasadena.com) features collections by 100 area designers and artists: build-your-own butterfly kits, steampunk gizmos and much more. Get a coffee fix at Pasadena's best source, Copa Vida.

❺ Asian Arts

In a stately 1920s Chinese Imperial Palace–style building, the **USC Pacific Asia Museum** (pacificasiamuseum.usc.edu; P ♿) has a deep collection of Japanese paintings, graphic illustrations, Buddhist and Hindu masterpieces and Chinese ceramics.

❻ Dinner and a Show

Sample fine California cuisine at the art deco–inspired **Bistro 45** (bistro45.com; P), followed by theater at the historic **Pasadena Playhouse** (pasadenaplayhouse.org) or comedy at the **Ice House** (icehousecomedy.com). If it's daytime, go straight to **Car Artisan Chocolate Cafe** (https://carartisanchocolate.com) for the best chocolate croissant you'll ever have.

Explore ◈
Burbank &
Universal City

Home to many of LA's major movie studios – including Warner Bros, Disney and Universal – the sprawling grid of suburbia known as the Valley is where the masses live. It's more laid-back and less walkable than other areas in the city, but there are good reasons to visit.

The Short List

○ **Universal Studios Hollywood (p160)** *Thrilling to the theme park built next to the movie studio of* Frankenstein *and* Jurassic Park.

○ **Warner Bros Studio Tour (p164)** *Touring the famous studio responsible for* Casablanca *and* Batman.

○ **Sushi Row (p166)** *Delighting in the dozens of sushi bars in Studio City that compete to deliver the best in raw fish and Japanese dishes.*

Getting There & Around

Ⓜ Take the Metro Line B (Red) from Downtown LA and Hollywood to Universal City/Studio City and the North Hollywood Stations.

🚗 When Dionne Warwick sang 'LA is a great big freeway...' she could have been describing the Valley.

Neighborhood Map on p162

Top Experience 📷

Find Thrills with Movie-Themed Fun at Universal Studios Hollywood

Although Universal is one of the world's oldest continuously operating movie studios (since 1912), it's best known for the theme park in and around the studio's backlot. The park has remained a draw for generations of visitors and locals alike, thanks to an entertaining, ever-changing mix of thrill rides and live-action shows.

◉ MAP P162, E5

universalstudios
hollywood.com

Ⓟ 🚻

Wizarding World of Harry Potter

At Universal's biggest attraction (expect long queues), climb aboard the **Flight of the Hippogriff** roller coaster and the 3-D **Harry Potter and the Forbidden Journey**. Buy wizarding equipment and 'every-flavour' beans in the fantasy-themed shops then dig into a feast platter with frosty mugs of butterbeer at **Three Broomsticks** restaurant.

Other Top Universal Attractions

The newest area in the park is **Super Nintendo World**. Within this gaming-themed zone, the big ride is **Mario Kart: Bowser's Challenge**, which uses virtual reality to put riders inside the game. Elsewhere, the **Jurassic World** ride is a float back to dinosaur days before a tumble through a land of raptors and T. rexes. **Revenge of the Mummy** is a short (but thrilling) indoor roller-coaster romp through Imhotep's Tomb that at one point has you going backwards and hits speeds of up to 45mph. A ride based on **The Simpsons** sends guests rocketing along with the Simpson family to experience a side of Springfield previously unexplored.

    The theme park also includes the original **tram tour of the studio backlot**, although over the years this has morphed into more of a theme-park ride than an actual behind-the-scenes tour.

Universal CityWalk

Flashing video screens, oversized facades and garish color combos (think Blade Runner meets Willy Wonka) animate **Universal CityWalk** (city walkhollywood.com; 👫), the outdoor shopping concourse adjacent to Universal Studios. Under the glitz, CityWalk's 65 shops, restaurants and entertainment venues will be familiar to anyone who has visited a US suburban mall.

★ **Top Tips**

o Budget a full day to see Universal, especially in summer.

o To beat the crowds, get there before the gates open or invest in the Universal Express pass or the guided VIP Experience.

o Buying tickets online often yields discounts.

o If you're arriving by subway, a free shuttle connects the park and Universal City station and saves a slog up a steep hill.

✕ **Take a Break**

There are plenty of dining choices at Universal CityWalk or we suggest heading to Ventura Blvd's Sushi Row, where you can splurge or have sneaky-good, affordable Japanese cooking at Daichan (p166).

Burbank & Universal City Universal Studios Hollywood

For reviews see

⦿	Top Experiences	p160
⊙	Sights	p164
✕	Eating	p164
🍷	Drinking	p165
🎭	Entertainment	p167
🔒	Shopping	p167

W Burbank Blvd

North Hollywood

Chandler Blvd

Chandler Blvd

NORTH HOLLYWOOD

North Hollywood Park

Weddington St

Magnolia Blvd

Vineland Ave

W Magnolia Blvd

Otsego St

NoHo Arts District

Colfax Ave

Hollywood Fwy

Bakman Ave

Lankershim Blvd

Clean Ave

Addison St

Riverside Dr

Camarillo St

Ventura Fwy

Ventura Fwy

Riverside Dr

Moorpark St

Hollywood Fwy

Lankershim Blvd

Cahuenga Blvd

Asanebo

Colfax Ave

Tujunga Ave

Arch Dr

Ventura Blvd

Universal City/ Studio City

Ventura Blvd

Kazu Sushi

Daichan

STUDIO CITY

Laurel Canyon Blvd

Mulholland Dr

0   1 km
0   0.5 miles

E   F   G   H

W Burbank Blvd

Chandler Blvd

MAGNOLIA PARK

Whinall Hwy

N Orchard Dr

1

N Keystone St

Clybourn Ave

W Magnolia Blvd

16

N Florence St

N Niagara St

N Frederic St

N Pass Ave

N Hollywood Way

Verdugo Park

W Verdugo Ave

N Buena Vista St

W Olive Ave

Oak St

2

Clark Ave

BURBANK

N California St

N Avon St

Camarillo St

W Alameda Ave

3

Johnny Carson Park

Riverside Dr

5

Pass Ave

Olive Ave

Ventura Fwy

Buena Vista Park

Warner Bros Studio Tour

1

Warner Bros Studios

Forest Lawn Memorial Park – Hollywood Hills

2

4

Valley Spring Lane

Toluca Lake

Lakeside Country Club

Los Angeles River

Forest Lawn Dr

Griffith Park

Universal Studios Hollywood

UNIVERSAL CITY

Barham Blvd

Burbank Peak (1690ft)

Cahuenga Peak (1820ft)

5

Hollywood Fwy
Cahuenga Blvd W

6

E   F   G   H

9

Sights

Warner Bros Studio Tour

TOUR

1 ⊙ MAP P162, G4

This tour offers a fun, mostly authentic look behind the scenes of a major movie studio. The two-hour standard tour kicks off with a video of WB's greatest hits *(Rebel Without a Cause, Harry Potter)*, before a tram whisks you around 110 acres of sound stages, legacy sets like *Friends* and the *Big Bang Theory*, and technical departments, including props, costumes and a collection of Batmobiles.

Tour variations include the Classics Tour, which focuses on the studio's history and production of films like *Casablanca* and the lengthy Deluxe Tour, which includes an in-depth guided tour. (wbstudiotour.com)

Forest Lawn Memorial Park – Hollywood Hills

CEMETERY

2 ⊙ MAP P162, H4

Pathos, art and patriotism rule at this humongous cemetery next to Griffith Park. A fine catalog of celebrities, from Lucille Ball and Bette Davis to Nipsy Hussle and Cindy Williams, rests within the manicured grounds strewn with paeans to recent North American history. (forestlawn.com; P)

NoHo Arts District

NEIGHBORHOOD

3 ⊙ MAP P162, C2

North Hollywood (NoHo) is where you find most of LA's acting and scriptwriting schools and scores of charmless studio apartments filled with people trying to realize their dreams. It also boasts over 20 stage theaters in 1 sq mile and a community of galleries, restaurants and vintage-clothing stores. (nohoartsdistrict.com)

Eating

Chili John's

AMERICAN $

4 ✕ MAP P162, F1

Seen in *Once Upon a Time in Hollywood*, this neighborhood institution has been dishing out chili around a U-shaped counter since 1946. It's most popular served over spaghetti, but it'll do chili dogs, sandwiches such as the Sloppy John (think Sloppy Joe with chili) and the open-faced Messy Marv. Chili comes in beef, chicken and vegetarian versions, mild to hot. (https://order.toasttab.com/online/chili-johns; P ♿)

Bob's Big Boy

DINER $

5 ✕ MAP P162, F3

Bob, that cheeky, pompadoured kid in red-checkered pants, hasn't aged a lick since serving his first double-decker burger almost a century ago. This Wayne

McAllister–designed, Googie-style 1949 coffee shop is the oldest remaining location of the once-nationwide burger chain. It serves a diner menu of classics. (bobs.net; P ♿)

Republic of Pie   PIES $

6 ✖ MAP P162, C2

Both sweet fruit and savory meat pies star at this reclaimed-wood-built shop in the NoHo Arts District. It's got all the standard comfort-food pies and quiches, and it pushes the envelope with creations such as chocolate banana and Earl Grey cream pies. The Republic also serves good sandwiches plus coffee and tea drinks, and it has sidewalk seats. (republicofpie.com; ♿)

Tuning Fork LA   CALIFORNIAN $$

7 ✖ MAP P162, A4

Using fresh produce from the nearby Studio City Farmers Market, this casual bistro defines the California cuisine ethos: fresh, simple and creative. The wine list is inspired with regional choices and the craft beer list is long. There's a music industry vibe here – CBS Studios are down the block – and staff spin tunes most nights. (https://tuningforkla.com)

Drinking

Amp Coffee LA   COFFEE

8 ☕ MAP P162, C2

Great little coffee bar in NoHo with a post-industrial cement-wall vibe. Excellent baked goods like banana

NoHo Arts District

Sushi Row's Japanese Delights

Those in the know come to the Valley for their sushi. In fact, Ventura Blvd in Studio City has so many excellent outlets that it's called Sushi Row. Among the great choices is **Daichan** (Map p162, C5; ☎818-980-8450; Ⓟ). Tucked away in an unassuming mini-mall, stuffed with knickknacks, pasted with posters and staffed by a sunny owner, this offbeat, home-style Japanese diner offers amazing deals. Fried seaweed tofu *gyōza* (dumplings) are divine and so are the bowls.

Other good options include upscale **Asanebo** (Map p162, A4; asanebo-restaurant.com; Ⓟ), another strip mall standout thanks to dishes such as halibut sashimi with fresh truffle, and *kanpachi* (amberjack) with miso and chilies. Chef Tetsuya Nakao has earned a Michelin star and helped launch chef Nobu Matsuhisa toward his Nobu restaurant empire. **Kazu Sushi** (Map p162, B5; kazusushi818.com; Ⓟ) calls a nondescript, split-level mini-mall home. It's one of the best-kept secrets among LA's sushi aficionados. Kazu Sushi is high-end, has a terrific sake selection and is worth the splurge for the much-praised *omakase* (chef's choice) course.

bread go down well with the long list of hot and cold drinks. Budding scriptwriters, nascent music producers and other burgeoning creative types try to line deals at the tables inside and out. There are rehearsal spaces in the back. (instagram.com/ampcoffeela)

Tony's Darts Away
CRAFT BEER

 9 🍺 MAP P162, H1

This old-shoe-comfy neighborhood bar is renowned for its extraordinary beer selection – there's a changing choice of 40 California craft beers on tap, plus wines and ciders. The food menu features sausages in many shapes and sizes plus myriad vegan options. There's a dart board, pool table, oodles of board games and delightful outdoor seating. (tonysda.com)

Black Market Liquor Bar
BAR

10 🍺 MAP P162, A5

Under a vaulted brick ceiling, this upscale neighborhood tavern has a menu of Bloodys (Mary with vodka, Maria with tequila, hell with gin), make-your-own mimosas, unusual cocktails and offbeat beers. They go great with sharing plates such as lobster rolls and meatballs with garlic crisps, plus Italian and American mains. Good brunch. (blackmarketliquorbar.com)

Club Cobra

LGBTIQ+

11 🚇 MAP P162, D1

Wearing its pride boldly outside where large rainbows adorn the walls, Club Cobra has three bars, a dance floor and regular shows that range from drag nights to go-go. It's renowned for its Thursday trans nights, Transfix. Always a fab time. (clubcobrala.com)

Velvet Martini Lounge

LOUNGE

12 🚇 MAP P162, B4

This sophisticated, intimate spot offers a night out with a mid-century vibe. Folks dress up for fine cocktails and entertainment that might include comedians like Patton Oswalt or jazzy combos. Theme nights celebrate champagne and other upscale treats. Food comes from the long-running Vitello's Restaurant out front (classic Italian). Reserve ahead when top acts are appearing. (vitellos restaurant.com)

Entertainment

Baked Potato

JAZZ, BLUES

13 ⭐ MAP P162, D5

Near Universal Studios, a winsome dancing spud beckons you inside this diminutive jazz-and-blues hall – LA's oldest – where the schedule mixes no-names with big-timers. Drinks are stiff, and vittles include ...yup, baked potatoes in two dozen flavors. Maple ham and corn anyone? (thebakedpotato.com)

El Portal

THEATER

14 ⭐ MAP P162, C2

The stage of this one-time vaudeville house from 1926 has been graced by headliners from Debbie Reynolds to Smokey Robinson and Carol Channing to James Corden. Restored to its former glory and now boasting a top sound system, it's a mainstay of the NoHo Arts District. Shows run on three stages. (elportaltheatre.com)

Zombie Joe's Underground Theatre

THEATER

15 ⭐ MAP P162, C3

Part theater, part haunted house, Zombie Joe's presents shows that are at turns creepy, campy, Goth, killer-thriller, deranged, downright jump-out-of-your-pants scary and (paradoxically?) well respected. Edgar Allen Poe is this NoHo venue's Shakespeare. (zombie joes.com)

Shopping

It's a Wrap!

CLOTHING

16 🔒 MAP P162, F1

This industry legend is the outlet for used on-screen wardrobes and props. Besides the cachet, you get great prices on mainstream designer labels. Suits are a steal, as is the denim. New merchandise arrives daily and items are racked by show affiliation. Near Halloween, there are special displays of authentic costumes from productions. (itsawraphollywood.com)

Worth a Trip 🔭

Check Out the Beauty & Beautiful People at Malibu

Everyone needs a little Malibu. Here's a moneyed yet laid-back beach town and celebrity enclave that rambles for 27 miles along the Pacific Coast Hwy, blessed with the stunning natural beauty of its coastal mountains, pristine coves, wide sweeps of golden sand and epic waves.

Getting There

🚌 The I-10 Fwy merges into the scenic Pacific Coast Hwy (Rte 1) at Santa Monica.

🚍 Metro's Malibu Express Line 134 leaves from downtown Santa Monica.

Getty Villa

Stunningly perched on an ocean-view hillside, the replica 1st-century Roman **Getty Villa** (getty.edu; P 🚹) is an exquisite, 64-acre show-case for Greek, Roman and Etruscan antiquities, in galleries, courtyards, lush gardens and the brain-bending Hall of Colored Marbles.

Malibu Pier

The **pier** (malibupier.com; P) marks the beginning of Malibu's commercial heart. It's open for strolling and license-free fishing and delivers fine views of surfers riding waves off Surfrider Beach (pictured).

El Matador State Beach

El Matador (californiabeaches.com/beach/el-matador-state-beach/; P) is arguably Malibu's most stunning beach. Stroll down the bluffs to sandstone rock towers that rise from emerald coves, where sunbathers walk through the tides and dolphins breech beyond the waves. Just east, **Zuma Beach** (https://beaches.lacounty.gov/zuma-beach; P) is more famous and has bus access from Santa Monica.

Nobu Malibu

The Malibu outpost of mega-celebrity chef Nobu Matsuhisa's empire of luxe Japanese restaurants, **Nobu Malibu** (noburestaurants.com/malibu; P), is consistently one of LA's hot spots, with a high A-lister quotient. It's a cavernous, modern wood chalet with sushi bar, dining room and patio overlooking the Pacific surf.

★ Top Tips

o Unless you strike gold and find free parking on the Pacific Coast Hwy, parking lot rates can be pricey.

o Malibu is best explored midweek; you'll have the roads and beaches mostly to yourself.

o Virtually all of California's beaches are open to the public. Even when access appears to be blocked by gated enclaves, the sands are yours to enjoy.

✕ Take a Break

Whitewashed dining rooms at **Malibu Farm Restaurant at the Pier** (malibu-farm.com) make for beachy keen munching on farm-to-table brunches, pizzas and sandwiches.

Worth a Trip 🔭

Don't Miss the Disneyland® Resort

Possibly California's most iconic sight, Walt Disney's illustrious creation is the self-dubbed 'Happiest Place on Earth.' The streets here are always clean, employees (aka 'cast members') always upbeat and parades happen every day. Since opening in 1955, the ever-growing Disneyland Resort has thrilled, enchanted and even confounded millions, who venture to Anaheim from around the globe.

Getting There

🚗 Anaheim is 25 miles southeast of Downtown LA on the I-5 Fwy.

🚆 Amtrak or Metrolink trains stop at Anaheim's ARTIC transit center and a shuttle ride to Disneyland on bus Routes 14 or 15.

Disneyland Park

Main Street USA

Fashioned after Walt's hometown of Marceline, Missouri, bustling **Main Street USA** resembles the classic turn-of-the-20th-century, all-American town. complete with barbershop quartet, penny arcades, ice-cream shops and the steam **Disneyland Railroad**. The latter is a great intro to the park as it circles the perimeter on its relaxed journey.

Great Moments with Mr Lincoln, a 15-minute audio-animatronic presentation on Honest Abe, sits inside the fascinating **Disneyland Story** exhibit, while kids love seeing early Disney cartoons like *Steamboat Willie* inside **Main Street Cinema**. Main Street ends in the **Central Plaza**, lorded over by the iconic **Sleeping Beauty Castle**, featured on the Disney logo.

Star Wars: Galaxy's Edge

Inside Disneyland's most recent and largest 'land' (14 acres), the thrilling **Star Wars: Rise of the Resistance** puts you and other members of the Resistance in the midst of an immersive adventure where you're captured by storm troopers and must escape from a Star Destroyer. Nearby are opportunities to make your own lightsaber or droid, or drink adult beverages or blue milk at **Oga's Cantina**, modeled after the inside of Jabba's Palace. Fans of the movies will enjoy the fanatical attention to detail.

Tomorrowland

The 1950s imagineers' vision of the future could now be called Mid-Century Land. Venerable **Space Mountain** remains one of the USA's best roller coasters, hurtling you into complete darkness at great speed. **Star Tours: The Adventures Continue**, is a *Star Wars*-themed ride that clamps you into a Starspeeder shuttle for a wild, 3D cruise around the galaxy.

For retro high-tech, the **monorail** glides from Downtown Disney and the hotels to its stop in

★ Top Tips

◦ Disneyland Resort has three main areas: Disneyland Park, Disney California Adventure (DCA), and Downtown Disney, an outdoor pedestrian mall.

◦ Download the Disneyland app to check ride status, buy admission tickets and make Genie+ and dining reservations.

◦ The cost of admission to Disneyland is based on demand. If you have flexibility, look for the days when there are fewer people.

◦ Parking costs $30 a day. Of the various ginormous parking structures, Pixar Pals puts you a pleasant stroll away from the parks, saving the need to line up for shuttles.

✕ Take a Break

There's no shortage of restaurants inside the resort; Downtown Disney offers dining for before, during or after your visit. Keep your ticket for re-entry to the parks.

There's some kind of parade at least once daily in Disneyland and DCA, with floats gliding down Disneyland's Main Street USA accompanied by favorite Disney tunes and costumed characters. Parades change seasonally. Don't miss DCA's premier show, the 22-minute **World of Color**.

Tomorrowland. Kiddies will want to jump aboard the **Finding Nemo Submarine Voyage** to look for the world's most famous clownfish.

Fantasyland

Though it's filled with characters of classic children's stories, Fantasyland's best known for '**it's a small world**,' a boat ride past hundreds of audio-animatronic children from a world of cultures all singing an ear-worm of a theme song. Another classic, the **Matterhorn Bobsleds**, is the park's original – and still fun – roller coaster. Sweet-natured **Snow White's Enchanted Wish** is a regularly updated affirmation of positive feelings.

Mr Toad's Wild Ride is a loopy jaunt in an open-air jalopy through London. Younger kids love whirling around the **Mad Tea Party** teacup ride, then cavorting with characters in nearby **Mickey's Toontown**.

Frontierland

This Disney 'land' recalls colonial Americana: the relaxing Mississippi-style paddle-wheel **Mark Twain Riverboat** and the 18th-century replica **Sailing Ship Columbia**. Thrills are provided by **Big Thunder Mountain Railroad**, a mining-themed roller coaster. Nearby is **Pirate's Lair on Tom Sawyer Island**, a non-tech throwback to the park's early days.

New Orleans Square

Honoring Walt's favorite city, New Orleans Square captures a slice of French Quarter charm. The ever-wonderful **Pirates of the Caribbean** is the longest ride in Disneyland (17 minutes) and provided inspiration for the popular movies. Over at the **Haunted Mansion**, 999 'happy haunts' – spirits, goblins, shades and ghosts – appear and evanesce while you ride in a cocoon-like 'Doom Buggy.' Nearby, a new ride called **Tiana's Bayou Adventure**, inspired by *The Princess and the Frog*, is set to open in 2024. Another newcomer, **Tiana's Palace**, is winning raves for its authentic New Orleans cuisine.

Adventureland

Loosely deriving its jungle theme from Southeast Asia and Africa, Adventureland has a number of attractions, but the hands-down highlight is the safari-style **Indiana Jones Adventure**. Cool down on the purposely hokey **Jungle Cruise**, viewing audio-animatronic animals. The classic **Enchanted Tiki Room** features carvings of Hawaiian gods and goddesses and a campy show of singing, dancing audio-animatronic birds and flowers. Skip the over-hyped Dole Whips.

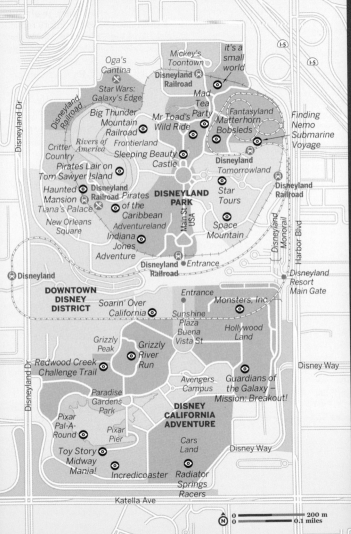

Oga's
Cantina

Mickey's
Toontown

it's a
small
world

Disneyland
Railroad

Star Wars:
Galaxy's Edge

Mad
Tea
Party

Disneyland
Railroad

Big Thunder
Mountain
Railroad

Mr Toad's
Wild Ride

Fantasyland
Matterhorn
Bobsleds

Finding
Nemo
Submarine
Voyage

Critter
Country

Rivers of
America

Frontierland

Sleeping Beauty
Castle

Pirates Lair on
Tom Sawyer Island

Disneyland

Tomorrowland

Haunted
Mansion

Disneyland
Railroad

Pirates
of the
Caribbean

Star
Tours

Disneyland
Railroad

Tiana's Palace

Adventureland

New Orleans
Square

Indiana
Jones
Adventure

DISNEYLAND
PARK

Space
Mountain

Disneyland Monorail

Harbor Blvd

Disneyland
Railroad

Entrance

Disneyland
Railroad

Disneyland

DOWNTOWN
DISNEY
DISTRICT

Entrance

Monsters, Inc

Disneyland Resort
Main Gate

Soarin' Over
California

Sunshine
Plaza

Buena
Vista St

Hollywood
Land

Grizzly
Peak

Grizzly
River
Run

Disney Way

Disneyland Dr

Redwood Creek
Challenge Trail

Avengers
Campus

Guardians of
the Galaxy –
Mission: Breakout!

Paradise
Gardens
Park

DISNEY
CALIFORNIA
ADVENTURE

Pixar
Pal-A-
Round

Pixar
Pier

Cars
Land

Toy Story
Midway
Mania!

Disney Way

Incredicoaster

Radiator
Springs
Racers

Katella Ave

Disneyland Dr

Main St USA

0   200 m
0   0.1 miles

Disney California Adventure

Across the plaza from Disneyland, **Disney California Adventure (DCA)** is an ode to California's geography, history and culture. Opened in 2001, DCA covers more acres than Disneyland, is very attractive and has a unified design that's more immersive than the original Disneyland Park. It feels less crowded and has excellent rides and attractions.

Hollywood Land & Avengers Campus

Hollywood's factory of dreams is presented here in miniature, with soundstages, movable props, and – of course – a studio store. **Guardians of the Galaxy – Mission: Breakout!** is the newest thrill ride, a tower with drops of 130ft through an elevator shaft. The less adventurous can navigate a taxicab through 'Monstropolis' on the **Monsters, Inc: Mike & Sulley to the Rescue!** ride.

Grizzly Peak

Grizzly Peak is DCA's salute to California's natural and human achievements. Its main attraction, the superb **Grizzly River Run** takes you 'rafting' down a faux Sierra Nevada river – you will get wet. While fake flat-hatted park rangers look on, kids can tackle the **Redwood Creek Challenge Trail**, with its 'Big Sir' redwoods, wooden lookouts, rock slide and climbing traverses.

    Soarin' Over California is a virtual hang-gliding thrill ride that's a big air-kiss to the state. If you're hungry, the **Corn Dog Castle** has a grab-and-go hot link corn dog that's the best in the parks.

Disneyland® Resort entrance

Genie+ & Lightning Lanes

Lines for Disneyland Resort rides and attractions can be long, but the Genie+ scheme can make your visit more efficient – at a cost.

○ Purchase the Genie+ option via the Disneyland app. Use it to reserve entrance times for popular rides and attractions, which can reduce your time waiting in line.

○ Once inside the park, you can start reserving entrance times, but you are limited in how often you can make them, so you can't plan out your day all at once. Also, waits for reservation times mean that you may have inconvenient gaps between rides, precluding other activities in the interim.

○ Use the Lightening Lane at rides where you've reserved a spot. This lets you bypass most of the people in the regular line, although you still may end up waiting.

○ Like admission tickets, Genie+ has demand-based pricing (from $25 per person), so some days are cheaper than others. Note that the most popular rides (eg Star Wars: Rise of the Resistance) are not in the Genie+ scheme; to use the Lightening Lane for these, you need a separate pass (from $25).

Cars Land

This land gets kudos for its incredibly detailed design based on the popular Disney Pixar *Cars* movies. Top billing goes to the justifiably popular **Radiator Springs Racers**, a race-car ride that bumps and jumps around a track painstakingly decked out like a cartoon American West.

Pixar Pier

If you like carnival rides, you'll love Pixar Pier, designed to look like an amalgam of California's beachside amusement piers. The scream-inducing **Incredicoaster** hurdles along as fast as baby Jack-Jack. Just as popular is **Toy Story Midway Mania!** – a 4D ride where you earn points by shooting at targets while your carnival car swivels and careens through an oversize, old-fashioned game arcade. It's all overlooked by **Pixar Pal-A-Round**, a 15-story Ferris wheel where gondolas pitch and yaw in little loops as well as the big one; you can request a less vertigo-inducing seat instead.

Downtown Disney District

Connecting Disneyland's parks and hotels, this open-air pedestrian mall is a triumph of marketing, bursting with opportunities to drop cash in stores, restaurants and entertainment venues. For 2024, Downtown Disney is diversifying its food offerings with some promising newcomers: **Paseo** and **Centrico**, both created by Chef Carlos Gaytan, the first Michelin star–awarded chef born in Mexico; and **Din Tai Fung**, a branch of the hugely popular Taiwanese original.

Survival Guide

Before You Go — 178

Book Your Stay — 178

When to Go — 178

Arriving in Los Angeles — 179

Los Angeles International Airport — 179

Hollywood Burbank Airport — 180

John Wayne Airport — 180

Union Station — 180

Long-Distance Buses — 180

Getting Around — 180

Public Transportation — 180

Bicycles — 182

Car & Motorcycle — 182

Taxi & Rideshare — 182

Essential Information — 182

Accessible Travel — 182

Business Hours — 183

Electricity — 183

Emergency & Important Numbers — 183

Money — 183

Public Holidays — 184

Safe Travel — 184

Telephone Services — 185

Tourist Information — 185

Venice Skatepark (p123) ONEINCHPUNCH/SHUTTERSTOCK ©

Before You Go

Book Your Stay

○ LA is huge. Do your research before booking a room or house. Do you want to be within stumbling distance of hot-spot bars and clubs, near major cultural sites or by the ocean?

○ Unless you plan on driving (and spending lots of time in traffic), find a place close to major metro or bus routes.

○ Most neighborhoods popular with visitors have hotels in just about every price range. Expect to pay between $150 and $300 per night for a midrange room.

Useful Websites

Lonely Planet (lonely planet.com/hotels) Independent accommodations reviews and recommendations.

HotelTonight (hotel tonight.com) California-based hotelsearch app

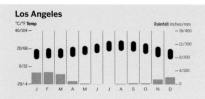

When to Go

Winter (Dec–Feb) Wettest season, though temperatures generally mild. Good hotel deals.

Spring (Mar–May) Ideal time to visit. Average rainfall drops dramatically by April; decent hotel deals; high demand in March due to the Academy Awards.

Summer (Jun–Aug) Peak tourist season; hot weather and big crowds. Outdoor concerts and beaches are at their best.

Autumn (Sep–Nov) Also ideal; warm temperatures and thinner crowds. Average rainfall remains low, especially in September.

offering lastminute bookings.

Vrbo (vrbo.com) Listings include houses, apartments and B&Bs.

Best Budget

HI Los Angeles – Santa Monica (hiusa. org) Budget-friendly digs that rival facilities at properties costing many times more.

Freehand (freehand hotels.com/los -angeles) Design-

literate dorms and private rooms in a hip Downtown hotel-hostel hybrid.

Samesun Venice Beach (samesun.com/ venice-beach-hostel) In a refurbished 1904 building with spectacular rooftop views of Venice Beach. Dorms and private rooms.

Best Midrange

NoMad Los Angeles (thenomadhotel.com/ los-angeles) Vintage interiors and a rooftop pool in a restored Downtown palazzo.

Silver Lake Pool & Inn (palisociety.com/hotels/silverlake) Laid-back boutique chic, steps away from hip eateries, bars and shops.

Seaview Inn (theseaviewinn.com) Low-key motel with a variety of rooms close to the sand in Manhattan Beach.

Best Top End

Sunset Tower Hotel (sunsettowerhotel.com) A striking West Hollywood icon rich in showbiz history.

Malibu Beach Inn (malibubeachinn.com) Coveted art, ocean views and interiors that make interior designers rave.

Shutters on the Beach (shuttersonthebeach.com) A New England–style retreat in Santa Monica.

Hollywood Roosevelt (thehollywoodroosevelt.com) Hollywood lore lives large at its most famous hotel (tip: get a pool room).

Arriving in Los Angeles

Los Angeles International Airport

LAX (flylax.com) is the city's main gateway, with nine terminals including Tom Bradley International Terminal, the hub for most international air carriers.

○ Terminals are linked by the free LAX Shuttle A, leaving from the lower (arrivals) level of each terminal. Hotel and car-rental shuttles stop here as well. The ADA Shuttle for travelers with disabilities must be arranged through your airline.

○ Taxis and ride-sharing vehicles are located at the LAX-it (pronounced 'LA Exit') stand, about a three-minute walk east of Terminal 1. A free, frequent shuttle bus connects all terminals to LAX-it.

○ **LAX FlyAway** (flylax.com/flyaway-bus) buses travel nonstop to Downtown's Union Station (35 minutes to one hour) and Van Nuys (40 minutes to one hour). Trip times are subject to traffic conditions.

○ For scheduled bus services, catch the free shuttle bus (labeled 'Lot South/City Bus Center') from the airport terminals to the LAX City Bus Center. From here, local buses serve LA County. For Santa Monica or Venice, change to the Santa Monica **Big Blue Bus** (bigbluebus.com) Line 3 or Rapid 3. If you're headed for Culver City, catch **Culver City Bus** (culvercitybus.com) Line 6 or Rapid 6.

○ LAX rail service includes the new Metro K Line (Pink) that includes the LAX/Metro Transit Station, set to open in late 2024. The new station will be linked to LAX by a new Automated People Mover (APM) which will serve the terminals and the new rental car center. In the meantime, if you want to catch a Metro train service, take the free Metro C (Green) Line shuttle bus from the terminals to Aviation/LAX station and then transfer to the Metro C (Green) Line light rail.

Hollywood Burbank Airport

Has extensive domestic and intra-California service from all major airlines. **Hollywood Burbank** (hollywood burbankairport.com) is convenient to Hollywood, Downtown LA and Pasadena.

John Wayne Airport

Located in Santa Ana in Orange County, **John Wayne Airport** (ocair.com) is close to the Disneyland Resort. It has extensive domestic and intra-California service from all major airlines.

Union Station

Interstate trains on Amtrak (amtrak.com) and regional Metrolink trains serve Downtown's historic **Union Station** (unionstation la.com).

Long-Distance Buses

The main bus terminal for **Greyhound** (grey hound.com) is in a bleak part of Downtown; try not to arrive after dark. Other discount bus lines such as FlixBus stop along Downtown streets that are subject to change.

Getting Around

Public Transportation

○ Most public transportation is handled by **Metro** (metro.net), which offers fare info, maps, schedules and trip-planning help.

○ To ride Metro trains and buses, buy a reusable TAP card. Available from TAP vending machines at Metro stations with a $2 surcharge, the cards allow you to add cash value. There are daily and weekly caps on fares, making them the equivalent of day and weekly passes.

○ Both single-trip tickets and TAP cards loaded with a day pass are available on Metro buses (ensure you have the exact change).

○ TAP cards are accepted on DASH shuttles and municipal bus services and can be reloaded at vending machines or online on the TAP website (taptogo.net).

Metro Rail

The Metro Rail network consists of two subway lines and four light-rail lines. Four lines converge in Downtown LA where there are two subway tunnels, one for the B and D lines and a new one for the A and E lines.

The most useful lines for visitors are:

A Line (Blue) Light-rail line running Pasadena to Long Beach; via Highland Park and Downtown.

B Line (Red) The most useful for visitors. A subway linking Downtown's Union Station to North Hollywood (San Fernando Valley) via central Hollywood and Universal City.

D Line (Purple) Subway line between Downtown LA, Westlake and Koreatown. The line's extension will see it reach Beverly Hills, Century City and Westwood in time for the 2028 Olympics (they hope).

E Line (Gold) Light-rail line linking East LA to Santa Monica via Downtown, Exposition Park and Culver City. It connects to the new K Line (Pink), which serves LAX, at the Expo/Crenshaw station.

Most lines run from around 4am or 5am to around 1am Sunday to Thursday, and until around 2:30am on Friday and Saturday nights. Frequency ranges from up to every five minutes in rush hour to every 10 to 20 minutes at other times.

Metro Buses

Metro operates dozens of bus lines across the city and offers three types of bus services:

Metro Local buses (painted orange) Make frequent stops along major thoroughfares throughout the city.

Metro Rapid buses (painted red) Stop less frequently and

have special sensors that keep traffic lights green when a bus approaches.

Metro Express buses (painted blue) Commuter oriented buses that connect communities with Downtown LA and other business districts and usually travel via the city's freeways.

Other Local Buses

o Santa Monica–based **Big Blue Bus** (bigblue bus.com) serves much of western LA, including Santa Monica, Venice and Westwood. Its weekday express bus 10 runs from Santa Monica to Downtown ($2.50, one hour).

o The **Culver City Bus** (culvercitybus.com) runs services throughout Culver City and the Westside.

DASH Buses

These small shuttle buses, run by the LA Department of Transportation (ladottransit. com), operate along 30 routes and serve local communities, but only until around 6:30pm to 7pm and with limited services on weekends. Many

lines connect with other DASH routes as well as Metro rail stations.

Some of the most useful routes include:

Beachwood Canyon Useful for close-ups of the Hollywood Sign; runs from Sunset Blvd up Vine St to Hollywood Blvd and Beachwood Dr.

Downtown Five separate routes hit all the hot spots. Route A runs from Little Tokyo to City West, Route B connects Chinatown to the Financial District, Route D travels between Union Station and South Park, Route E connects City West to the Fashion District, and Route F connects the Financial District to Exposition Park and USC.

Fairfax Makes a handy loop past the Beverly Center mall, western Melrose Ave, the Farmers Market/Grove and Museum Row.

Hollywood Covers Hollywood east of Highland Ave and links with the short Los Feliz Route at Franklin Ave and Vermont Ave.

Observatory/Los Feliz Runs from Vermont/Sunset metro station

(B Line) to Griffith Observatory, running north along Vermont Ave en route and south on Hillhurst Ave on the way back.

Bicycles

Los Angeles and the region have a growing network of bike lanes and cyclists are well-accommodated.

o Metro operates a region-wide bikeshare system called **Metro Bike** (bikeshare.metro.net).

o Bikes can be brought onto Metro buses and trains at all times.

o BikeLA has a great collection of online bike lane maps and more at la-bike.org/bike-maps.

Car & Motorcycle

o Having your own wheels is useful for exploring many parts of Southern California, although this means contending with some of the worst traffic in the country. Traffic jams can even occur after midnight. Avoid rush 'hour' (7am to 10am and 3pm to 7pm).

o Parking at a few hotels and motels may be free; however, most places charge parking rates – some hefty. Short-term rental apartments may come with parking, which is a huge convenience. Valet parking at pricier restaurants is commonplace.

o All familiar car-rental companies have branches at the airports and throughout LA; some companies rent electric or hybrid vehicles.

Taxi & Rideshare

o Because of LA's size and traffic, getting around by cab or rideshare will cost you.

o Cabs are best requested over the phone, though some prowl the streets late at night. They are always lined up at the airports, Union Station and major hotels.

o Taxi companies include **LA City Cab** (lacitycab.com).

o Ridesharing companies Uber (uber.com) and Lyft (lyft.com) are extremely popular. Many visitors use Metro trains ands buses, augmented by rideshares, for their entire time in LA.

Essential Information

Accessible Travel

o Los Angeles is generally well equipped for travelers with disabilities.

o All transit companies in the LA metro area offer wheelchair accessible services and travel discounts for travelers with disabilities. Major car-rental companies can usually supply hand-controlled vehicles with one or two days' notice.

o Telephone companies provide free relay operators (dial 711) for the hearing impaired.

o Many banks have ATM instructions in braille.

o For more information, download Lonely Planet's free Accessible Travel guide from https://shop.lonely planet.com/categories/accessible-travel or check out the following resources.

A Wheelchair Rider's Guide to the California Coast (wheelingcalscoast.org) Free online directory and downloadable guide for LA and Orange County coasts, covering wheelchair access at beaches, parks and more.

Guide to Accessibility in Los Angeles (discoverlosangeles. com/travel/the-guide-to-accessibility-in-los-angeles) Offers information on accessible sightseeing, entertainment, museums and transportation.

Society for Accessible Travel & Hospitality (TTY; sath.org)

Business Hours

Banks 9:30am–6pm Monday to Friday, some 9am–2pm Saturday

Bars 4pm–2am daily

Business hours (general) 9am–5pm Monday to Friday

Post offices 9am–5pm Monday to Friday, some 9am–1pm Saturday

Restaurants 7:30am–10:30am, 11am–3pm & 5:30pm–10pm daily, some later Friday and Saturday

Shops 10am–7pm or later Monday to Saturday, noon–6pm Sunday (malls stay open later)

Supermarkets 7am–10pm daily

Electricity

Type A
120V/60Hz

Type B
120V/60Hz

Emergency & Important Numbers

Ambulance, fire or police ☏911

Country code ☏1

International dialing code ☏011

Operator ☏0

Directory assistance ☏411

Money

Most people don't carry large amounts of cash for everyday use, relying instead on contactless payments as well as credit and debit cards. Some businesses refuse to accept any cash or bills over $20.

ATMs

o ATMs are available 24/7 at banks, shopping malls, airports and grocery and convenience stores.

o Expect a minimum surcharge of around $3 per transaction, in addition to any fees charged by your home bank.

o Withdrawing cash from an ATM using a credit card usually incurs a hefty fee.

Changing Money

You can exchange money at major airports and currency-exchange offices such as LA Currency (la currency.com). Simply getting US currency from an ATM is often the cheapest option, even with fees.

Credit Cards

It's impossible to rent a car, book a hotel room or buy tickets online without a credit card.

Taxes & Refunds

o The California state sales tax of 7.25% is added to the price of most goods and services. Local city sales taxes may add up to 2.75% more.

o No refunds of sales or lodging taxes are available for international visitors.

Tipping

Airport skycaps & hotel bellhops $2 per bag, minimum $5 per cart.

Bartenders 15% per round, minimum $2 per drink.

Concierges Nothing for simple information; $20 or more for securing last-minute restaurant reservations, sold-out show tickets etc.

Housekeeping staff $2 to $5 daily.

Parking valets At least $2 when handed back your car keys.

Restaurant servers & room service 20% or more, unless a gratuity is already charged (common for groups of six or more).

Taxi drivers 10% to 15% of metered fare, rounded up to the next dollar.

Public Holidays

On the following national holidays, banks, schools and government offices (including post offices) close, and transportation, museums and other services operate on a Sunday schedule. Holidays falling on a weekend are usually observed the following Monday.

New Year's Day January 1

Martin Luther King Jr Day Third Monday in January

Presidents' Day Third Monday in February

Memorial Day Last Monday in May

Juneteenth June 19

Independence Day July 4

Labor Day First Monday in September

Columbus Day/ Indigenous Peoples' Day Second Monday in October

Veterans Day November 11

Thanksgiving Day (Fourth Thursday in November)

Christmas Day December 25

In addition, Black Friday, the day after Thanksgiving, is a day of retail madness and sales. It's a holiday for many.

Safe Travel

Despite its seemingly apocalyptic list of dangers – guns, violent crime, earthquakes – Los Angeles is a reasonably safe place to visit. The greatest danger is posed by car accidents (buckle up – it's the law), while the biggest annoyance is sclerotic traffic.

Earthquakes happen all the time, but most are so tiny they are detectable only by sensitive instruments. If you are caught in a serious temblor:

o If indoors, get under a sturdy desk or table and cover your head and neck with your arms. If in bed, stay in bed and cover your head and neck with a pillow.

o Stay clear of windows, mirrors or anything that might fall.

o Don't head for elevators and never go running into the street.

o If you're in a shopping mall or large public building, expect the alarm and/or sprinkler systems to come on.

o If outdoors, get away from buildings, trees, power lines or anything that might fall.

o If you're driving, pull far over to the side of the road away from bridges, overpasses and power lines. Stay inside the car until the shaking stops.

o If you're on a sidewalk near buildings, duck into a doorway to protect yourself from falling debris.

o Prepare for aftershocks. Check online if possible for updates.

Telephone Services

o US phone numbers consist of a three-digit area code followed by a seven-digit local number. Always dial all 10 digits.

o For international visitors, a US prepaid rechargeable SIM card is usually cheaper than using your home network.

o SIM cards are sold at phone and electronics stores (buy eSIMs online). These stores also sell inexpensive prepaid phones.

Tourist Information

LA's tourism office, **Discover LA**, operates a comprehensive website (discoverlos angeles.com) and app.

Beverly Hills Visitors Center (Map p78, B5; lovebeverlyhills.com; 🛜) Sightseeing, activities, dining and accommodations information focused on the Beverly Hills area.

Santa Monica Visitor Information Center (santamonica.com) The main tourist information center in Santa Monica; also has an office on the pier.

Visit West Hollywood (Map p78, F2; visitwest hollywood.com; 🛜) Online info on attractions, accommodations, tours, LGBTIQ+ topics and more in the West Hollywood area.

Behind the Scenes

Send Us Your Feedback

We love to hear from travelers – your comments help make our books better. We read every word, and we guarantee that your feedback goes straight to the authors. Visit **lonelyplanet.com/contact** to submit your updates and suggestions.

Note: We may edit, reproduce and incorporate your comments in Lonely Planet products such as guidebooks, websites and digital products, so let us know if you are happy to have your name acknowledged. For a copy of our privacy policy visit **lonelyplanet.com/legal**.

Ryan's Thanks

Huge thanks go out to all my LA pals, especially the great Adam Skolnick, who paved a smooth path for me. At Lonely Planet, thanks to Sarah Stocking for this surprise of a dream gig. And to Alexis, who stars in all my dreams.

Acknowledgements

Cover photographs: (front) Fireworks over downtown Los Angeles, LPETTET/Getty ©; (back) Downtown Los Angeles, pablopicasso/Getty ©
Photographs pp32–3: (clockwise from top left) Oscity/Shutterstock ©; 4kclips/Shutterstock ©; Let Go Media/Shutterstock ©

This Book

This 7th edition of Lonely Planet's *Pocket Los Angeles* guidebook was researched and written by Ryan Ver Berkmoes. The 5th and 6th editions were written by Cristian Bonetto and Andrew Bender, and the 4th edition was written by Adam Skolnick. This guidebook was produced by the following:

Destination Editor
Sarah Stocking

Product Editor
Katie Connolly

Cartographer
Julie Sheridan

Book Designer
Nicolas D'Hoedt

Editor Christopher Pitts

Cover Researcher
Kat Marsh

Thanks to Ronan Abayawickrema, Clare Healy, Karen Henderson, Kate James, Amy Lysen

Index

See also separate subindexes for:

⊗ **Eating** p190

⊝ **Drinking** p190

✪ **Entertainment** p191

⊡ **Shopping** p191

Index

6th Street Viaduct 146

A

Abbot Kinney Boulevard 127
Academy Museum of Motion Pictures 92-3
accessible travel 182-3
accommodations 178-9
activities 22, see also individual activities
Ahmanson Theatre 152
ambulance 183
Angels Flight 147
Angels Point 67
Annenberg Community Beach House 112
architecture 81, 89, 93, 105, 139, 145
area codes 183
art galleries 44
ATMs 183
Autry Museum of the American West 60

Sights 000
Map Pages 000

B

Ballerina Clown 125
Baywatch 114
beaches 24, 109, 125, 134-5, 169
Bergamot Station Arts Center 112
Beverly Hills, see West Hollywood & Beverly Hills
Beverly Hills Experience 82
bicycling 20, 182
  Bike Center Santa Monica 113
  Bikes & Hikes LA 82
  Marvin Braude Bicycle Trail 109
  Venice 130
Biddy Mason Memorial Park 146-7
Bike Center Santa Monica 113
Bikes & Hikes LA 82
Binoculars Building 127-8
Birth of Venus mural 127
Bo Bridges Gallery 135
Bob Baker Marionette Theater 71
books 17, 53, 65, 87, 132, 153

Bradbury Building 146
Broad 138-9
Bronson Canyon 60
Bruce's Beach 135
budget 30
Burbank & Universal City 159-67, **162-3**
  drinking 165-7
  entertainment 167
  food 164-5, 166
  nightlife 165-7
  shopping 167
  sights 160-1, 164
  transportation 159
bus travel 181-2
business hours 183

C

California African American Museum (CAAM) 155
California Heritage Museum 112-13
California Science Center 155
Capitol Records 43-4
car travel 182
Carroll Ave 67
CBS Television City 99-100
celebrity spotting 25, 82
cell phones 30, 185

Chateau Marmont 82
children, travel with 18-19
climate 178
comedy clubs 85
costs 30
Cove Skatepark 114
Craft Contemporary 99
credit cards 184
Culver City 104-5, **104**
Culver Hotel 105
Culver Studios 105
currency 30
cycling, see bicycling

D

dangers 184-5
disabilities, travelers with 182-3
Disney California Adventure 174-5
Disneyland Park 171-2
Disneyland® Resort 170-5, 173
Dolby Theatre 39
Dorothy Chandler Pavilion 152
Downtown 137-53, **142-3**
  drinking 150-1
  entertainment 151-2
  food 147-9
  nightlife 150-1

Downtown (continued)
shopping 152-3
sights 138-9, 144-7
transportation 137
walks 140-1, **140**
dress codes 48
drinking & nightlife 14-15, see also Drinking subindex, individual neighborhoods
driving 182

E

earthquakes 185
Eastern Columbia Building 141
Echo Park 66-7, **66**
Echo Park Lake 67
Edgemar 113
Egyptian Theatre 44
El Matador State Beach 169
El Pueblo de Los Ángeles Historical Monument 145
electricity 183
emergencies 183
entertainment, see also Entertainment subindex, individual neighborhoods
events 27
Exposition Park 154-5

F

family travel 18-19
fashion 16
festivals 27

fire 183
food 12-13, 149, see also Eating subindex, individual neighborhoods
food trucks 12
Forest Lawn Memorial Park - Hollywood Hills 164
Frederick R Weisman Art Foundation 80

G

galleries 44
Gamble House 157
gay travelers 27, 84
Genie+ 175
Getty Center 88-9
Getty Villa 169
Gold's Gym 127
Grammy Museum 144-5
Grand Central Market 148
Greystone Mansion & Gardens 81-2
Griffith Observatory 56-7
Griffith Park 60
Griffith Park, Silver Lake & Los Feliz 55-65, **58-9**
drinking 62-3
entertainment 63-5
food 60-2
nightlife 62-3
shopping 65
sights 56-7, 60
transportation 55

H

Hancock Park 100
Heal the Bay Aquarium 112

Highland Park 69-75, **70**
drinking 72-3
food 71-2
nightlife 72-3
shopping 73-5
sights 71
transportation 69
Highland Park Bowl 71
highlights 6-11
hiking 47, see also walks
Hispanic culture 75
history 133
holidays 184
Hollyhock House 60
Hollywood 37-53, **40-1**
drinking 47-50
entertainment 50-3
food 44-7
nightlife 47-50
shopping 53
sights 38-9, 42-4
transportation 37
Hollywood Forever Cemetery 42
Hollywood Museum 39
Hollywood Walk of Fame 38-9

I

internet resources 178-9
itineraries 28-9
Culver City 104-5, **104**
Downtown 140-1, **140**
Echo Park 66-7, **66**
Manhattan Beach 134-5, **134**
Pasadena 156-7, **156**
Venice 124-5, **124**

J

James Oviatt Building 141
Japan House 43
Japanese American National Museum 145
Japanese Art Pavilion 95
Jim Morrison mural 127
juice 14

K

Kidspace Children's Museum 157
Kirk Douglas Theatre 105
Kohn Gallery 44
Koreatown 99

L

La Brea Tar Pits & Museum 98-9
LA Louver 127
LACMA 94-5
language 30
Leonard Nimoy Event Horizon Theater 57
lesbian travelers 27, 84
LGBTIQ+ travelers 27, 84
live music 23
Los Angeles Central Library 141
Los Angeles City Hall 146
Los Angeles County Museum of Art 94-5
Los Angeles Memorial Coliseum 155

Los Angeles Music Center 152

Los Angeles Police Museum 71

Los Feliz, *see* Griffith Park, Silver Lake & Los Feliz

Lucas Museum of Narrative Art 155

M

Madame Tussaud's 43

Malibu 168-9

Malibu Pier 169

Manhattan Beach 134-5, **134**

Mariachi Plaza 75

Marina Del Rey Parasailing 128-9

Mark Taper Forum 152

MGM Studios 105

Mid-City, *see* Miracle Mile & Mid-City

Millennium Biltmore Hotel 141

Miracle Mile & Mid-City 91-103, **96-7**

drinking 101-2

entertainment 102-3

food 99, 100-1

nightlife 101-2

shopping 103

sights 92-5, 98-9, 100

transportation 91

mobile phones 30, 185

MOCA Grand Avenue 144

money 30, 183-4

motorcycle travel 182

movie studios 50

Muscle Beach 123, 125

Museum of Jurassic Technology 105

Museum of Tolerance 80-1

N

Natural History Museum 155

nightlife 14-15, *see also* Drinking sub-index, individual neighborhoods

NoHo Arts District 164

Norton Simon Museum 157

O

Off the 405 89

opening hours 183

Original Muscle Beach 109

P

Pacific Design Center 81

Pacific Park 109

Palace Theatre 141

Palisades Park 112

Paramount Pictures 42

Pasadena 156-7, **156**

Petersen Automotive Museum 98

police 183

Poseidon 113

public holidays 184

public transportation 180-2

R

Real Los Angeles Tours 42

refunds 184

Regen Projects 44

responsible travel 20-1

ridesharing 182

Rodeo Dr 87

rooftop bars 150

Rose Bowl Stadium 157

Runyon Canyon 47

S

safety 184-5

Samuel Oschin Planetarium 57

Sand Dune Park 135

Santa Monica 107-19, **110-11**

drinking 117

entertainment 118-19

food 114-17

nightlife 117

shopping 119

sights 108-9, 112-14

transportation 107

Santa Monica Pier 108-9

Santa Monica Pier Carousel 109

Schindler House 81

shopping 16-17, *see also* Shopping sub-index, individual neighborhoods

Silver Lake, *see* Griffith Park, Silver Lake & Los Feliz

skateboarding 22, 114, 123

Sony Pictures Studios 50, 105

South LA 26

South Venice Beach 125

sports 151

Starry Night mural 127

street art 127

surfing 24

sushi 166

T

taxes 184

taxis 182

TCL Chinese Theatre 39

telephone services 30, 185

time 30

tipping 30, 184

TMZ Celebrity Tour 42

top experiences 6-11

tourist information 185

train travel 180-1

transportation 31, 179-82

travel seasons 178

trekking 47

U

under the radar LA 26

Union 76 Gas Station 81

Union Station 145

Universal City, *see* Burbank & Universal City

Universal Studios Hollywood 160-1

USC Pacific Asia Museum 157

V

vegan & vegetarian travelers 12, 67, 72, 82-3, 129, 148

Venice 121-33, **126**

drinking 130-1

food 129-30

history 133

nightlife 130-1

Venice (continued)
shopping 132-3
sights 122-3, 127-8
transportation 121
walks 124-5, **124**
Venice Beach Art Walls 123, 125
Venice Boardwalk 122-3, 125
Venice Canals 127
Venice Skatepark 123, 125
volleyball 24

W

walks 47
Culver City 104-5, **104**
Downtown 140-1, **140**
Echo Park 66-7, **66**
Manhattan Beach 134-5, **134**
Pasadena 156-7, **156**
Venice 124-5, **124**
Walt Disney Concert Hall 144
Warner Bros Studio Tour 50, 164
weather 178
websites 178-9
West Hollywood & Beverly Hills 77-87, **78-9**
drinking 84, 85
entertainment 84, 85-6
food 82-5
nightlife 85
shopping 86-7
sights 80-2
transportation 77

Sights 000
Map Pages **000**

Westlake 26
Whitley Heights 42-3
Wisdom Tree, Cahuenga Peak & Mt Lee Summit 47
Wizarding World of Harry Potter 161

⊗**Eating**

Ahgassi Gopchang 99
All Day Baby 60-1
All Time 61
Asanebo 166
Bar Amá 147
Bavel 147-8
Bay Cities Italian Deli & Bakery 116
Birdie G's 116
Bistro 45 157
Bob's Big Boy 164-5
Butcher, the Baker, the Cappuccino Maker 83
Butcher's Daughter, the 129
Cafe Birdie 72
Café Gratitude 129
Canter's 100
Car Artisan Chocolate Cafe 157
Cassia 114
Catch LA 82
Chili John's 164
Clark Street Diner 46
Clifton's Republic 141
Cole's 149
Craig's 84
Crossroads Kitchen 82-3
Daichan 166
Dogtown Coffee 109
Donut Friend 72
Eggslut 148
Élephante 115

Felix Trattoria 129
Figaro Bistrot 62
Gelateria Uli 149
Getty Center 89
Gjelina 129
Gjusta 129
Grandmaster Recorders 46
Holey Grail Donuts 116-17
Hollywood Farmers' Market 47
HomeState 61-2
Joe's Pizza 47
Joy 71
Kazu Sushi 166
Kitchen Mouse 72
Loqui 105
Luv2eat 47
Malibu Farm Restaurant at the Pier 169
Manhattan Beach Creamery 135
Mariscos El Faro 71
MB Post 135
Mélisse 114-15
Mercado 116
Mercado La Paloma 155
Milo & Olive 116
Mother Wolf 45
Musso & Frank Grill 44
Nate'n Al's 84
Nobu Malibu 169
Oaks Gourmet 47
Original Farmers Market 100
Orsa & Winston 149
Otium 139
Pazzo Gelato 62
Pearl River Deli 149
Petit Trois 45
Philippe the Original 149
Pine & Crane 61

Pink's Hot Dogs 101
Playita Mariscos 62
Prince 99
Providence 45
Queen St Raw Bar & Grill 72
Ramen Hood 148
Ray's 95
Republic of Pie 165
Republique 100
Rose 123
Sage 67
Salt & Straw 130
Santa Monica Farmers Markets 114
Santa Monica Seafood 115-16
Scoops 72
Sonoratown 148
Spago 83
Sunny Blue 115
Superba Food & Bread 130
Sushi Gen 148
Tacos 1986 100-1
Tail O' the Pup 85
Teddy's Red Tacos 129
Trails 57
Trejo's Coffee & Donuts 46
Tuning Fork LA 165
Villa Moreliana 148
Villa's Tacos 71
Wee Chippy, the 130

⊙**Drinking**

10 Speed Coffee 117
Abbey, the 84
Akbar 63
All Season Brewing Company 102
Amp Coffee LA 165-6
Bar Chloe 117
Bar Clara 150

Bar Lis 50
Be Bright Coffee 101
Big Bar 63
Black Market Liquor
    Bar 166
Brig 131
Burgundy Room 49
Chez Jay 117
Club Cobra 167
Covell 63
Dresden Lounge 62
Eagle LA 63
Eightfold Coffee 67
El Carmen 102
Endorffeine 150
EP & LP 85
Ercoles 135
ETA 73
Everson Royce
    Bar 150
Frolic Room 39
G&B Coffee 148
Gold Line 73
Ham & Eggs
    Tavern 151
Harvard & Stone 48
High Rooftop
    Lounge 130
Hinano Cafe 131
Homebound Brew
    Haus 145
Honey's at Star
    Love 48
Javista Hollywood
    47-8
Kumquat Coffee Co 72
La Cuevita 73
La Descarga 49
Library Alehouse 117
Maru Coffee 62
Melrose Umbrella Co
    101-2
Micky's 84
No Vacancy 49
Ototo 63

Penthouse 117
Perch 150
Polo Lounge 85
Precinct 151
Saint Felix 84
Sassafras Saloon 48
Tabula Rasa Bar 48
Tiki-Ti 63
Tony's Darts Away 166
Townhouse &
    Del Monte
    Speakeasy 131
Trunks 84
Upstairs at the Ace
    Hotel 150
Varnish 150
Velvet Martini
    Lounge 167
Venice Ale House
    130-1
Virgil 62
Waterfront 125

Entertainment

Aero Theater 118
Baked Potato 167
Broad Stage 118
Catalina Jazz Club
    52-3
Cinelounge Sunset 51
Comedy Store 85
Crypto.com
    Center 151
Dodger Stadium 64-5
Echo + Echoplex 64
El Capitan Theatre 52
El Portal 167
El Rey Theatre 102-3
Fonda Theatre 52
Greek Theatre 64
Groundlings 103
Harvelle's 118
Hollywood Bowl 50
Hollywood Pantages
    Theatre 51-2

Hotel Cafe 51
Ice House 157
Improv 85
Laemmle Monica
    Film Center 119
Largo at the
    Coronet 85
Laugh Factory 85
Los Feliz Theatre 64
New Beverly
    Cinema 103
Pasadena
    Playhouse 157
Rooftop Cinema Club
    DTLA 152
TCL Chinese
    Theatre 39, 51
United Artists
    Theatre 152
Upright Citizens
    Brigade Theatre 50
Vibrato Grill Bar 85-6
Vista Theatre 63-4
Whisky-a-Go-Go 86
Zombie Joe's
    Underground
    Theatre 167

Shopping

Amoeba Music 53
Arbor Venice 133
Avalon Vintage 74-5
Aviator Nation 132
Bay Cities Italian Deli
    & Bakery 116
Big Bud Press 74
Book Soup 87
Burro 132
Counterpoint 53
Dotter 75
Foxhole LA 65
Fred Segal 86
Galco's Old World
    Grocery 74
Gold Bug 157

Great Labels 119
Grove 103
Gucci Salon
    Melrose 86-7
It's a Wrap! 167
Jadis 119
JF Chen 53
Kingswell 65
Kiss Kiss Tattoo 132
Larry Edmunds
    Bookshop 53
Last Bookstore 153
Lemon Frog 65
Linus 130
Luxe de Ville 65
Main St 119
Matrushka 65
Melrose Avenue 103
Montana Ave 119
Mystery Pier
    Books 87
On Maritime
    Records 73-4
Principessa 133
Puzzle Zoo 119
Reformation 103
Row DTLA 152-3
Santa Monica
    Place 119
Santee Alley 153
Shorthand 75
Skylight Books 65
Slow 103
Small World
    Books 132
Stories 67
Strange Invisible
    Perfumes 133
Ten Women 119
Third Street
    Promenade 119
Universal
    CityWalk 161
Village Well Books 105
Wacko 65

Our Writer

Ryan Ver Berkmoes

Ryan Ver Berkmoes grew up in California and loved LA, even before there was a song. He has explored the region from top to bottom, from ocean to desert. Ryan has created his own tours of movie and TV locations and traced the footsteps of Philip Marlowe. When not seeking a new candidate for best donut, Ryan writes about travel the world over. @ryanvb

Published by Lonely Planet Global Limited
CRN 554153
7th edition – February 2024
ISBN 978 1 83869 132 5
© Lonely Planet 2024 Photographs © as indicated 2024
10 9 8 7 6 5 4 3 2 1
Printed in Malaysia